Williamson's directory, for the city of Edinburgh, Canongate, Leith, and suburbs; from June 1778, to June 1779. ...

Peter Williamson

ECCO
PRINT EDITIONS

Williamson's directory, for the city of Edinburgh, Canongate, Leith, and suburbs; from June 1778, to June 1779. ...

Williamson, Peter
ESTCID: T120276
Reproduction from British Library

Edinburgh : printed by P. Williamson, and sold at his Penny-Post Office, [1778].
[2],123,[5]p. ; 8°

Gale ECCO Print Editions

Relive history with *Eighteenth Century Collections Online*, now available in print for the independent historian and collector. This series includes the most significant English-language and foreign-language works printed in Great Britain during the eighteenth century, and is organized in seven different subject areas including literature and language; medicine, science, and technology; and religion and philosophy. The collection also includes thousands of important works from the Americas.

The eighteenth century has been called "The Age of Enlightenment." It was a period of rapid advance in print culture and publishing, in world exploration, and in the rapid growth of science and technology – all of which had a profound impact on the political and cultural landscape. At the end of the century the American Revolution, French Revolution and Industrial Revolution, perhaps three of the most significant events in modern history, set in motion developments that eventually dominated world political, economic, and social life.

In a groundbreaking effort, Gale initiated a revolution of its own: digitization of epic proportions to preserve these invaluable works in the largest online archive of its kind. Contributions from major world libraries constitute over 175,000 original printed works. Scanned images of the actual pages, rather than transcriptions, recreate the works *as they first appeared.*

Now for the first time, these high-quality digital scans of original works are available via print-on-demand, making them readily accessible to libraries, students, independent scholars, and readers of all ages.

For our initial release we have created seven robust collections to form one the world's most comprehensive catalogs of 18th century works.

Initial Gale ECCO Print Editions collections include:

History and Geography
Rich in titles on English life and social history, this collection spans the world as it was known to eighteenth-century historians and explorers. Titles include a wealth of travel accounts and diaries, histories of nations from throughout the world, and maps and charts of a world that was still being discovered. Students of the War of American Independence will find fascinating accounts from the British side of conflict.

Social Science

Delve into what it was like to live during the eighteenth century by reading the first-hand accounts of everyday people, including city dwellers and farmers, businessmen and bankers, artisans and merchants, artists and their patrons, politicians and their constituents. Original texts make the American, French, and Industrial revolutions vividly contemporary.

Medicine, Science and Technology

Medical theory and practice of the 1700s developed rapidly, as is evidenced by the extensive collection, which includes descriptions of diseases, their conditions, and treatments. Books on science and technology, agriculture, military technology, natural philosophy, even cookbooks, are all contained here.

Literature and Language

Western literary study flows out of eighteenth-century works by Alexander Pope, Daniel Defoe, Henry Fielding, Frances Burney, Denis Diderot, Johann Gottfried Herder, Johann Wolfgang von Goethe, and others. Experience the birth of the modern novel, or compare the development of language using dictionaries and grammar discourses.

Religion and Philosophy

The Age of Enlightenment profoundly enriched religious and philosophical understanding and continues to influence present-day thinking. Works collected here include masterpieces by David Hume, Immanuel Kant, and Jean-Jacques Rousseau, as well as religious sermons and moral debates on the issues of the day, such as the slave trade. The Age of Reason saw conflict between Protestantism and Catholicism transformed into one between faith and logic -- a debate that continues in the twenty-first century.

Law and Reference

This collection reveals the history of English common law and Empire law in a vastly changing world of British expansion. Dominating the legal field is the *Commentaries of the Law of England* by Sir William Blackstone, which first appeared in 1765. Reference works such as almanacs and catalogues continue to educate us by revealing the day-to-day workings of society.

Fine Arts

The eighteenth-century fascination with Greek and Roman antiquity followed the systematic excavation of the ruins at Pompeii and Herculaneum in southern Italy; and after 1750 a neoclassical style dominated all artistic fields. The titles here trace developments in mostly English-language works on painting, sculpture, architecture, music, theater, and other disciplines. Instructional works on musical instruments, catalogs of art objects, comic operas, and more are also included.

bibliolife

old books. new life.

The BiblioLife Network

This project was made possible in part by the BiblioLife Network (BLN), a project aimed at addressing some of the huge challenges facing book preservationists around the world. The BLN includes libraries, library networks, archives, subject matter experts, online communities and library service providers. We believe every book ever published should be available as a high-quality print reproduction; printed on-demand anywhere in the world. This insures the ongoing accessibility of the content and helps generate sustainable revenue for the libraries and organizations that work to preserve these important materials.

The following book is in the "public domain" and represents an authentic reproduction of the text as printed by the original publisher. While we have attempted to accurately maintain the integrity of the original work, there are sometimes problems with the original work or the micro-film from which the books were digitized. This can result in minor errors in reproduction. Possible imperfections include missing and blurred pages, poor pictures, markings and other reproduction issues beyond our control. Because this work is culturally important, we have made it available as part of our commitment to protecting, preserving, and promoting the world's literature.

GUIDE TO FOLD-OUTS MAPS and OVERSIZED IMAGES

The book you are reading was digitized from microfilm captured over the past thirty to forty years. Years after the creation of the original microfilm, the book was converted to digital files and made available in an online database.

In an online database, page images do not need to conform to the size restrictions found in a printed book. When converting these images back into a printed bound book, the page sizes are standardized in ways that maintain the detail of the original. For large images, such as fold-out maps, the original page image is split into two or more pages

Guidelines used to determine how to split the page image follows:

• Some images are split vertically; large images require vertical and horizontal splits.
• For horizontal splits, the content is split left to right.
• For vertical splits, the content is split from top to bottom.
• For both vertical and horizontal splits, the image is processed from top left to bottom right.

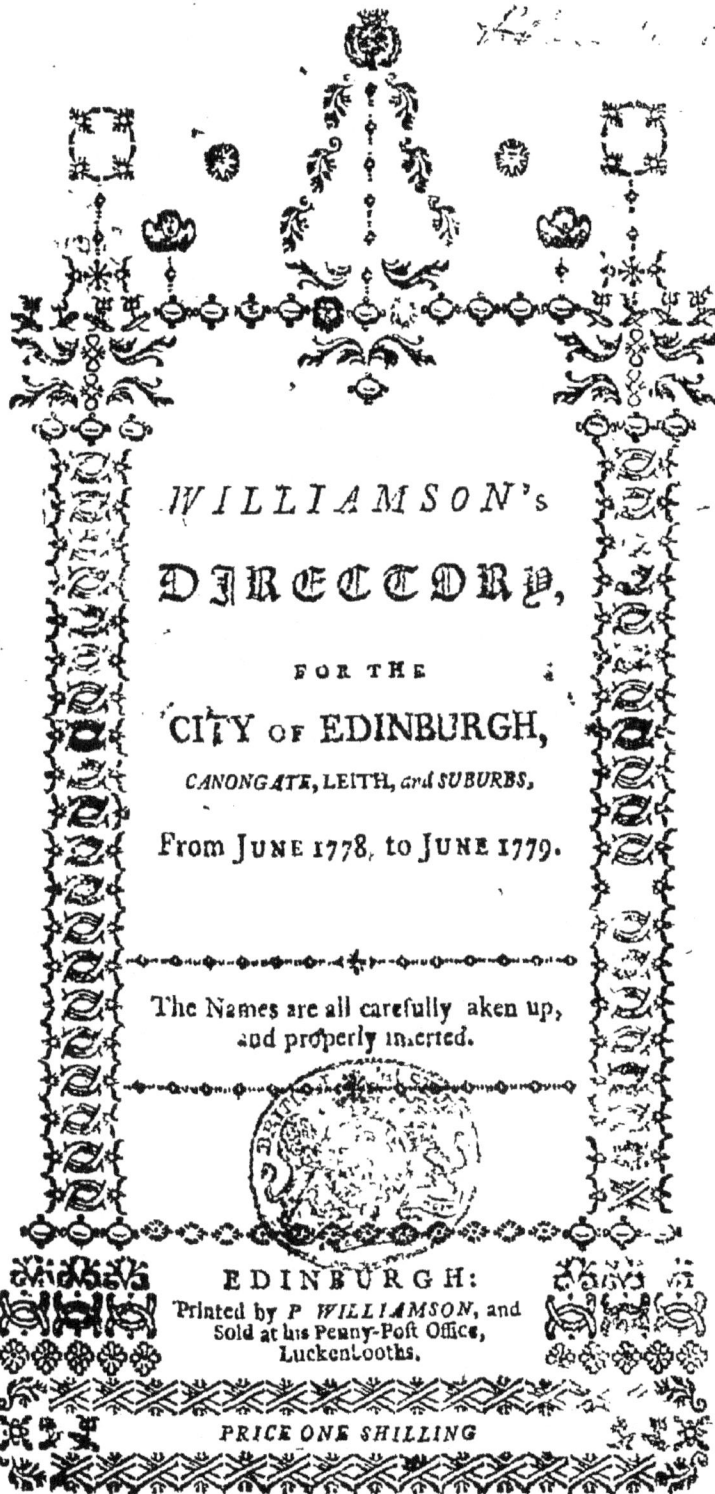

WILLIAMSON's
DIRECTORY,

FOR THE
CITY OF EDINBURGH,

CANONGATE, LEITH, and SUBURBS,

From JUNE 1778, to JUNE 1779.

The Names are all carefully aken up,
and properly inserted.

EDINBURGH:
Printed by P WILLIAMSON, and
Sold at his Penny-Post Office,
Luckenbooths.

PRICE ONE SHILLING

LIST of the Right Honourable the Lords of Council and Seffion.

Robert Dundas of Arnifton, Efq; Lord Prefident, Adams' court.
Thomas Miller of Barmfkming, Efq, Lord Juftice clerk Brown's fquare
Henry Home of Kaims, new ftreet, canongate
Alexander Bofwell, of Auchinleck, back of meadows
James Erfkine of Alva, Argyle's fquare
James Vietch, of Elliock. Jock's lodge
John Campbell, of Stonefield, George's fquare
Francis Garden of Gardenftone, at St Katherine's
Robert Bruce, of Kennet, Horfe wynd
Sir David Dalrymple of Hales, new ftreet, canongate
James Burnet of Montboddo, St John's ftreet
Alexander Lockhart of Covington, Adams' fquare
David Rofs of Ankerville, St Andrew's fquare
Robert M'Queen, of Braxfield, George's fquare
David Dalrymple, of weft-hall, advocates clofe

Henry Dundas, Efq. Lord Advocate, George's fquare
Alexander Murray, Sollicitor general, Brown's fquare

BARONS of EXCHEQUER

The Right Honourable James Montgomery, Lord chief baron, canongate
John Maul, Efq; nether-bow
John Grant, Efq: nether-bow
Fletcher Norton, Efq: new town.
Sir John Dalrymple, Nicolfon's ftreet
Sofmo Gordon, Efq; New town

to the Right Honourable

JOHN DALRYMPLE, Esq;   LORD PROVOST,

JAMES HUNTER, Esq;
THOMAS CLEGHORN, Esq;
GILBERT MEASON, Esq;   } BAILIES.
JAMES HOTCHKIS, Esq;

A N D,

TO THE OTHER MEMBERS OF THE

TOWN COUNCIL

OF THE

CITY OF EDINBURGH,

THIS DIRECTORY,

IN TESTIMONY OF THE HIGH ESTEEM

WHICH THE PUBLISHER HAS

FOR THAT

RESPECTABLE BODY,

IS

WITH THE GREATEST SUBMISSION

DEDICATED

BY THEIR MOST OBEDIENT

AND HUMBLE SERVANT

PETER WILLIAMSON.

WILLIAMSON's
DIRECTORY,

For the City of EDINBURGH, &c,

A Bercrombie James, general, George's square
Abercrombie George, advocate, Bristo street
Abercrombie Alex. writer to sig. Gosford's cl.
Abercrombie Alexander, advocate, president stairs
Abercrombie Mrs, calton-hill
Aberdeen William, grocer, at the crackling house
Aberdour James, founder, Miln's square
Abernethy Drummond William, physici. St John's hill
Abernethy John, writer, advocate's close
Abernethy James, grocer, cowgate-head,
Aboyne Earl of, St John's street
Achyndachy Alexander, advocate, Warriston's close
Adair Thomas, writer, James's court
Adam John, architect, Merlin's wynd
Adam Alex. rector of the high school, Crichton street
Adam Alexander, flater, lauriston
Adam Mrs, tin-plate worker, near the tolbooth can.
Adamson Archibald, taylor, cross cauley
Addison Mrs, chapel street
Adie John, shoe maker, west end of lauriston
Adie Mrs, grocer, foot of Libberton's wynd
Adie James merchant, grass market
Agnew Lady, Brown's square
Aikman Mrs, merchant, luckenbooths
Ainslie Philip, colonel, new street
Ainslie David, writer, bunker's hill
Ainslie John, land surveyor, parliament square]
Ainslie Miss, Gosford's close
Aitchison William, baxter, chapel street
Aitchison Alexander, jeweler, parliment square
Aitchison & Turnbull, watch-makers, b of city guard
Aitchison John, merchant, at the cross
Aitchison Mrs, midwife, below Chessels's court

Aitken Robert, writer, well bow foot
Aitke John grocer, cowgate head
Aitken John, furgeon, high fchool yards
Aitken Thomas, merchant, Herriot's bridge
Aitken John, bellows-maker, head of Gray's clofe
Aitken Mrs, mantua-maker, Libberton's wynd
Aitken john, grocer, Nicolfon's ftreet
Aitken Mifs, merchants, luckenbooths
Aitken Charles, wright, Currie's clofe, caftle-hill
Aitken Archibald, wright, tolbooth wynd cnongate
Aitken John, watch-maker, canongate-head
Aitken David, yarn manufacturer, potter-row
Aitken Mrs, thread maker, plainftone clofe, canong.
Aitkenhead Mrs, room-letter, grafs-market Side
Alexander William, joiner and cabinet maker, britto ftr
Alexander Mrs, pleafance
Alexander James harnefs-maker, watergate
Alexander Alex wright, Falconer's land. canongate
Alexander Walter, wright, Shakefpeare fquare
Alexander Walter, grocer, above the old bank clofe
Alexander Mr, mutton chop houfe, Forrefter's wy.
Alifon Alex, cafhier to the excife, Pirie's clofe, can.
Alifon Mifs, mantua maker, Monteith's clofe
Alifon Alexander, extractor, Miln's court
Alifon Mrs, New-ftreet
Alifon and Co, milliners, fountain clofe
Allan Mifs, caftle-hill
Allan John, minifter, back of the fountain well
Allan John, writer, Scot's clofe cowgate
Allan Thomas, merchant, canongate head
Allan and Stewart, bankers, writers court
Allan Robert, fun fire office, writers court
Allan Mrs, brewer, grafs-market
Allan Alexander, merchant, parliament fquare
Allan Mifs, milliner, oppofite the guard
Allan William fchool-mafter, luckenboths
Allan Henry, baxter, cowgate-head
Allan Charles, barber, grafs-market
Allan and Lauruton, haberdafhers, parliament fquare
Ales Alexander, taylor Mint
Alfton Mrs, room letter, Strichen's clofe
Alfton Mrs, Weir's clofe, canongate

Alſton John, toy-merchant, front of the exchange
Alſton Gavin, printer, old fiſh market cloſe
Alſton Miſs, mantua-maker, writers court
Al.. Phil, major, in the caſtle
Al.. Thomas depute clerk of tiends, Tiend office
A.... Mrs, Monteith's cloſe
Anderſon Francis, writer to the ſignet, Carrubber's cl.
Anderſon William, ſurgeon, Kincaid's land, cowgate
Anderſon Mrs Hyndford's cloſe
Anderſon David, writer to the ſignet, Carrubber's cl.
Anderſon Mrs, Blackfriars wynd
Anderſon William, wigmaker pleaſance
Anderſon Charles, writer Forreſter's wynd
Anderſon W ſen. writ... g. Buchanan's court
Anderſon William, cl... cuſtom houſe, Hamilton's folly
Anderſon John, brewer, north back of cowgate
Anderſon James, wigmaker after, h of Blackfriars wy.
Anderſon Mrs, new ſtreet
Anderſon Robert, feed-merchant, oppoſite the croſs
Anderſon Robert, merch. lawn-market N. ſide
Anderſon Mrs, merchant, luckenbooths
Anderſon William, iron-monger, weſt bow
Anderſon William, ſaddler, cowgate-head
Anderſon Mrs, hatter, new bank cloſe
Anderſon John, copper ſmith, weſt bow
Anderſon James, grocer, head of Chalmers' cloſe
Anderſon James, grocer, graſs-market
Anderſon John, eſq. advocate, Brown's ſquare
Anderſon Mrs, potter row
Anderſon Archibald, ſuperviſor, Middleton's entry
Anderſon Mrs, grocer, head of covenant cloſe
Anderſon Mrs, Nicolſon's ſtreet
Anderſon Mrs, Skinner's cloſe
Anderſon Mrs, china merchant, Stricher's cloſe
Anderſon Patrick, bookſeller parliament ſquare
Anderſon John, cork cutter, foot of Stevenlaw's cl.
Anderſon John, baker, calton
Anderſon John, ſpirit-dealer, Patterſon's court
Anderſon James, ſhoemaker, St Andrew's ſtreet
Anderſon William, ſhoe-maker, Leith wynd
Anderſon James, ſhoe-maker, goole dub
Anderſon Henry, ſhoe maker, front of Wardrope's c.

Anderson Robert, upholsterer, cowgate-foot
Anderson George, wig maker, lawn-market
Anderson James, hair-dresser, Leith wynd
Anderson Mrs, mantua-maker, Miln's court
Anderson David, taylor, canongate-head
Anderson Mrs, room-letter, op Queensberry's lodg.
Anderson Mrs, room letter, Patterson's court
Andrew George, waiter, Miln's square
Andrew John, grocer, front of James' court
Andrew Mrs, grocer, covenant close head
Andrew Mrs, Stonelaws close
Angelo Tremamendo fencing master, Nicolson's str.
Angus Colin, foot of the cross causey
Angus James, lock-smith, St Ninian's row
Annandale Mrs, room-letter, Miln's court
Anstruther Mrs of Inverkeithing, bishops land
Anstruther John, Esq advocate, Brown's square
Anstruther Mrs, Brown's square
Arbuthnot Mill, fountain bridge
Arbuthnot Robert, and Co. merchants, exchange
Archer George,   , Forrester's wynd
Archibald Joseph, sells all kinds of plants Charles' str.
Archibald William, grocer, portsburgh
Archibald Thomas, school master, portsburgh
Archibald William, slater, chapel of ease
Archibald Thomas, vintner, candle-maker row
Armour John, taylor, advocate's close
Armstrong David, advocate, middle meal-market stairs
Armstrong William, copper-smith, west-bow
Armstrong Francis, merchant, lockenbooths
Armstrong Mrs, founder, castle-wynd
Armiston Lady, George's square
Arret and Williamson, surgeons, Gray's close
Arnot Hugo, advocate, prince's street, new town
Arnot James, brewer, abbey
Arnot William, baxter, oppos. canongate cau d'
Arnot David, smith, abbey hill
Arthur Mrs, baker, opposite Queensberry's lodging
Arthur James, surgeon, Charle's street
Arthur Frederick, druggist, chapel street
Auchinleck Mrs, of Woodcockdale, old fish market cl.

Auchinleck Gilbert, cutler, nether-bow
Auchinleck John, smith, St Ninian's row
Aughterlony John, silk dyer, Blackfriar's wynt
Auld Robert, writer, back stairs
Auld George, goldsmith, silver mills
Auld William, locksmith, Shakespeare square
Austin Mrs, St David's street
Aytons Miss, of Canada, lady Stair's close
Aytons Miss, bishop's land close
Ayton Robert, founder, calton
Ayton W. writer to the sig above Balfour's coffee-ho.

B

Babtee John, vintner, covenant close
Baill Robert, society
Baillie William, advocate, James' court
Baillie Matthew, stabler, at the west port
Baillie Alexander, shoe-maker, grass market
Baillie Thomas, writer to the signet, James' court
Baillie James, writer, Carrubber's close
Baillie Miss, north Gray's close
Baillie James, baxter, at the canongate church
Baillie Mrs, Hyndford's close
Baillie Mrs, back of the guard
Baillie William, siennes
Baillie David, writer, Morrocco's close, canongate
Baillie Thomas, writer, old assembly close
Baillie Mrs, Libberton's wynd
Baillie David, writer, flesh-market close, canongate
Baillie John, Middleton's entry
Bain James, minister, Nicolson's street
Bain William, wright, St Ninian's row
Bain James, land surveyor, abbey
Bain Peter, wright, Nicolson's street
Bain John, letter founder, calton
Bain James, shoe-maker, Gunstone's close cowgate
Bain George, clerk to Sir John Ingles, Alison's sq.
Bain Daniel, vintner, old fish market close
Bain Alexander, wright, Potter-row port
Bain George, keeper of John's coffee house, parli. sq.
Bain Captain, royal navy, new street
Baird Thomas, King's park
Baird James, grocer, grass-market

Baird Thomas, lockſmith, Auld's cloſe, cowgate.
Baird James, painter, cowgate-head
Baird James, writer, Stonelaw's cloſe
Baird John, writer, Nicolſon's ſquare
Baird Miſs at Newbyth, chapel ſtreet
Baird James phyſician, north Gray's cloſe
Bairnsfeth George, plumber, abbey hill
Bairnsfather George, brewer, back of the canongate
Balcarras lady, Dickſon's cloſe
Balcarras Counteſs of, S John's ſtreet
Baird Mrs, room-letter, writers court
Balfour James, eſq. at Pilrig
Balfour John, merchant, prince's ſtreet
Balfour Robert, ſhoe-maker, graſs market, S ſide
Balfour John, book-ſeller, at the croſs
Balfour David, writ at Mr Leith's taylor, prince's ſtr.
Balfour John, ſurgeon, Carrubber's cloſe
Balfour Mrs, Pirie's cloſe canongate
Balfour Mrs, Somerville's cloſe canongate
Balfour Mrs, Henderſon's ſtairs
Balfour Andrew, Middleton's entry
Balfour James, Charles' ſtreet
Balfour James, writer, Advocates cloſe
Balfour James, writer to the ſignet, Argyle's ſquare
Balfour Andrew, advocate, Fiſher's cloſe, lawn market
Balling David, captain of city guard, Gosford's cl.
Ballantyne Mrs, pewterer, cowgate-head
Ballantyne John, merchant, weſt bow head
Ballantyne Alexander, copper-ſmith, weſt bow
Ballantyne James, writer, back of the guard
Ballantyne James, wheel-wright, canongate-head
Ballantyne James, ſhoe-maker, Richmond ſtreet
Ballantyne Mrs room-letter, plaſance
Ballantyne William, watch-maker, foot the pleaſance
Ballantyne James, writer, Roxburgh's cloſe luckenb.
Balmain james, ſolicitor of exciſe, w. end of lauriſton
Balmain John, cloſet keeper, Duty's office, caſtle hill
Banks Mrs, room-letter, weſt-bow head
Banantyne Andrew, bankers clerk, calton hill
Banantyne Miſs, milliner, back of the fountain well
Banantyne Mrs, milliner, blackfriars wynd
Banantyne Miſs, ſociety

Bannerman George, grocer, abbey
Bannerman William, taylor, calton
Barclay Henry, Esq. advocate, Carrubber's close
Barclay Anthony, writer to the signet, James' court
Barclay W. sec. to annexed estates, Cheffels' c. can.
Barclay William, grocer, canongate head
Barclay George, cutler, portsburgh
Barclay Alexander, hatter, pleafance
Barclay William, taylor, advocates close
Barclay Mrs, room-fetter, bull turnpike
Barclay Robertson, writer to the signet St John's street
Barclay Mrs. mantua-maker, Chalmers' close
Barret William, doctor, broughton
Barr Robert, grocer, cowgate-head
Barrie Alexander, English teacher, Jackson's close
Bartlet Benjamin, store-mafter, castle
Bartlet Mrs, head of Chalmers' close
Barrowman Will ——— ——— head of new street
Barr ——— ——— canongate foot
Barron James, ——— ———, canongate foot
Baron James, brewer, potter-row
Barron William, hair-dreffer, foot of Forrester's wy.
Bathgate George, meffenger. foot of Forrester's wy.
Baxter John, architect, prince's street
Bayll John, vintner, bridge street
Beakie Lady, Niddrey's wynd
Beath John, shoe maker, calton
Beath Thomas, writer. hammermen's close, canongate
Beatson Andrew, merchant, weft-bow-head
Beatson David, hofier, front of exchange
Beatson John, merchant, luckenbooths
Beatson David-Bofwel, Buccleugh street
Beech Patrick, goldsmith, Chrichton's street
Begg Allen, accomptant of excife, Charles's street
Begbie Adam, taylor, potter-row
Begbie Joseph, hatter, St Ninian's row
Begbie George, smith, weft bow
Begbie George, baxter, head of Halkerston's wynd
Begrie Robert, grocer, pleafance
Begrie John, vintner, oppofite the tolbooth
Bellches John, advocate, foot of Niddrey's wynd

Belsches Sir John, advocate, Nicolson's square.
Belsches Thomas, writer, new bank close
Belsches Mrs, Nicolson's street
Bell Robert, minister, Chrichton's street
Bell William, minister, Brown's close
Bell Adam, writer, upper baxter's close
Bell Hamilton, writer Wardrop's court
Bell .... , Kincaid's land, cowgate
Bell Andrew, engraver, lawnston
Bell .... James, printers Merlin's wynd
Bell .... , writer, wind mill street
Bell .... , solicitor's clerk, Charles street
Bell .... , Duncan's land, canongate
Bell John, bookseller, parliament square
Bell Andrew, baxter, head of the pleasance
Bell Alexander, merchant, head of Gosford's close
Bell Andrew, cooper, canongate foot
Bell Mrs, grocer, canongate
Bell Andrew, barber, luckenbooths
Bell Bartholomew and Hugh, brewers, pleasance
Bell Andrew, smith, canongate-head
Bell James, smith, cross causey
Bell William, taylor, potter-row
Bell .... , and P. Morison's taylor, James' court
Bell Thomas, candle-maker, cross-causey
Bell Andrew, cross causey
Bell Mrs, Middleton's entry
Ben .... , surgeon, Nudery's wynd
Ben .... David, clerk in the post office, Nidrey's wynd
Ben .... , merchant, new street
Ben .... , wig-maker, bull wynd
Ben .... , grocer, back of the grind
Ben .... John, wright, canon
Ben .... Campbell, writer, Gibb's close canong
Ben .... Robert, advocate, Alison's square
Ben .... , St Andrew's street
Ben .... , seal cutter, head of Baddery's wynd
Ben .... James, cage-maker, calton
Bertram William, wine merchant, fountain bridge
Bertram James, merchant, grass market
Bertram, Gardner and Co. merchants, exchaarge

Berwick Robert, grocer front of Buchanan's court
Besile and Dickson, masons, bristo-street
Bethune Mrs, St Mary wynd
Bengo Gavin, coach painter, St Agnes street
Beveridge James, writer, St Andrew's street
Beveridge Mrs, boarder, Nicolson's square
Beverly Alex, uph lst bridge fr h Shakespeare 'sq.
Biggar John, Walker and Co. linen manufact heads
Biggar Mrs, canongate head
Binny Mrs, hatter, t ct of Bordwick's close
Binning William, advocate, west-bow foot
Binning Mrs, abbey close
Binney Miss, Well's close, canongate
Bisset Andrew, writer at h Carlile's, Shakespea e sq.
Bisset Robert, shoe maker, St Mary's row
Bishop James, g ather, gilbet toll
Blacketer K. & E. milliners, bridge street
Blacklock Thomas, minister, Crichton's street
Blackwood Mrs of Petreavie, James's court
Blackwood Alexander, shoe-maker, calton
Black John, merchant, luckenbooths
Black John, shoe-maker Warriston's close
Black Mrs, Skinners close
Black Ludovick, shoe maker, Halkerston's wynd
Black Daniel, breeches-maker, bristo port
Black Robert, shoe maker, potter-row
Black Mrs, Nicolson's street
Black Joseph, physician, Argyle's square
Black John, grocer, head of Blackfriars wynd
Blackey Mrs, Middleton's entry
Blackhall Thomas, Dalrymple's office
Blackwood Mrs, Libberton's wynd
Blackwood Miss, Argyle's square
Blair John, brewer, abbey close
Blair Mrs, loom-setter, Geddes' close
Blair Mrs, north Gray's close
Blair of Balthagock, St John's street
Blair John, wright, castle-mill
Blair Mrs, lauriston
Blair James, wr to the signet, at A Giles, College wr
Blair Gilbert, barber, St Mary's wynd
Blair Thomas, writer, mint point

Blair Mrs, of Beltenmint, Chapel street
Blair Robert, advocate, Argyle's square
Blair Francis, linen manufacturer, luckenbooths
Blair William, writer, at Mr Grant's, Brown's sq.
Blair Hugh, doctor, Argyle's square
Blair Mrs, new street
Bland James, manager, theatre-royal, Gabriels row
Blane Andrew, writer to the signet, Brand's l. castle h.
Blane Mrs, teacher of English, Morrocco's close
Bramhall Baillie, saddler, head of covenant close
Blyth Miss, mantua-maker, west-bow
Blyth Robert, trunk maker, back of fountain well
Blyth James, taylor, plainstone close, canongate
Borg Andrew, cutler, Leith wynd
Boog William, taylor, Peebles wynd
Boggs Mrs, room-setter, opposite bowhead well
Boggue John, writer, Shakespeare square
Boggue Mrs, room-setter, back of the canongate
Brechtston Mrs, Nicolson's street
Bol. David clerk in the excheq Blackfriars wynd
Bonner Andrew, merchant, post office stairs
Bonnar David, cross-cauley
Bonnar J. dep. sollicitor of excise, Wilson's court can.
Bonnar John, painter, head of Niddery's wynd
Bonthron John grocer, pleasance
Bonthron David, mason, pleasance
Borthwick Mrs, Blair's close, castle-hill
Borthwick William, seedsman, advocates close
Borthwick Alexander, merchant, lawn market N. side
Borthwick Francis, stocking maker, New street, car.
Boswell James, advocate, James' court
Boswell Claud, advocate, Argyle's square
Boswell Robert, writer to the signet, princes street
Boswells Miss, Argyle's square
Boswell John, physician, St Andrew's square
Boswell Mrs. old post house stairs
Bosston Mrs, Nicolson's street
Bouchier   , Nicolson's street
Bower John, teacher of music, Brown's close, canong.
Bowie Mrs, Paxton's land, grass-market
Bowie Peter, accomptant, castle-hill
Bowie James, grocer, opposite the guard

Bowie Miffes, and Co merchants, luckenbooths
Bowie Mrs, auctioneer, Brodie's clofe
Bowie Ralph, writer, at Mrs M'Dowals Lawn market
Bowie Robert St Andrew's ftreet
Bow Peter, baker, back of the theatre
Bowen James, oyfter-cellar, Merlin's wynd
Bowman Charles, writer, tiend office, grafs-market
Bowman Mrs, foot of Niddery's wynd
Bowman John, efq, abbey
Boyd George, merchant, oppofite old bank clofe
Boyd Robert, writer, Paterfon's court
Boyd James, painter, canongate-head
Boyd Walter, wig-maker, head of Blackfriars wynd
Boyd Mrs, downmoft baxters clofe
Boyd James, ftabler, canongate-head
Boyd Cathcart, examiner of the cuftoms Jack's l. can.
Boyes Andrew, writer, J. Davidfon's caftle-hill
Boyle Mrs, room-fetter, poft-houfe ftairs
Boyter Alexander, grocer, oppo. tolbooth wynd can.
Brackenrig John, watch maker, portfburgh
Braidwood William, wright, Gifford's park
Braidwood Mrs, brifto-ftreet
Braidwood W. cl. to Alexander & Sons, lawn-market
Braidwood T. teacher of dumb people, St Leonard hill
Braidwood Francis, joiner, cabinet maker and Auc-
        tioner, Lady Stairs' clofe
Braidwood W. Iron monger & ftationer, grafs market
Brand Alexander, writer, Morrocco's clofe, canong.
Brafh James, taylor, Mills land
Breaden James, ftay-maker, weft end of lauriefton
Brichan Charles, wright, portfburgh
Bremner James, writer, Herriot's bridge
Bremner Robert, mufic-fhop, head of old affembly cl.
Bremner Hugh, writer, Hunter's clofe, grafs-market
Bremner Robert, ftamp office
Bremner James, meal maker, meal market
Bridges David, broad cloth merchant, luckenbooths
Bridges, David, vintner, bridge-ftreet
Bridges William, baxter, St Ninian's row
Brodie Mrs, of Lethem, St Andrew's fquare
Brodie and Son, wrights, lawn market

Brodie James, wright, near the crecl ing house
Brodie Mrs, castle-hill
Brodie Alexander, caster, back of the fountain well
Brodie James, Surgeon, head of Galloway's clofe
Brougham   , St Andrew's fquare
Broughton Edward, accomp. of excife, fountain bridge
Broughton Mrs, Richmond ftreet
Brough John, chandler, foot of Peebles wynd
Brough John, cork cutter, foot of Stonehiw's clofe
Brough John, cabinet maker, St Andrew's ftreet No 4
Brotherfone John, upholfterer, bell's wynd
Brotherfone Peter, carpet manufact, Richmond ftr.
Brown Charles, advocate, castle-hill
Brown John, merchant, cowgate head
Brown john, pewterer, grafs market fenth fide
Brown James, smith, west-bow
Brown Archibald, Efq; op. Crichton's entry canong.
Brown John, merchant, lawn market
Brown Matthew, doctor, Miln's court
Brown Alexander, bookfeller, above fhip clofe
Brown Robert, Nicolfon's ftreet
Brown Mifs, of Coultermains, two penny cuftom
Brown John, fhoe maker, portfburgh
Brown James, grocer, portfburgh
Brown George, commiffioner of excife, George's fq.
Brown Robert, grocer, lawn market
Brown William, druggift, weft bow
Brown Charles, writer to the fignet, Argyle's fquare
Brown Alexander, librarian, Kincaid's land cowgate
Brown William, boot-binder, Rattray's clofe cowg.
Brown Mrs, Charles' ftreet
Brown Mrs, Teviot row
Brown Robert, founder, Galloway's clofe lawn mark.
Brown Mrs, coffee houfe keeper, crofs
Brown Alexander, wine-merchant, Craig's clofe
Brown Samuel, watch-maker, oppofite the guard
Brown Mrs, faddler, bull turnpike
Brown James, ftay maker, Rea's clofe, canongate
Brown William, grocer, oppofite the fountan well
Brown Mrs, head of Kennedy's clofe
Brown John, watch-maker, head of Bell's wynd
Brown James, glover, oppofite tolbooth door

Brown Archibald, cutler, west port

Brown William, teacher of English, Carrubber's close

Brown James, architect, George' square

Brown James, mancher, In action

Brown George, shoemaker, behind the crackling house

Brown Thomas, taylor, bride-street

Brown Robert, grocer, broad-street

Brown James, wright, chapel street

Brown James, bookseller, parliament square

Brown Arch. wr fountain bridge, or town clerk's office

Brown James, butter and cheese office, west bow

Brown John, physician, tolnk close

Brown Miffes, milliners, Peebles wynd

Brown John, Iron monger, opposite the corn-market

Brown and Buchan, wrights, foot of Niddery's wynd

Brown John mason, Charles street

Brown James, jun. stay maker canongate-head

Brown Mis, Snakespear's square

Brownfield George, taylor, fountain close

Brownlee Mrs, Buchanan's court

Brownlees David, horse hirer, grass-market

Bruce Sir Michael, St Andrew's square

Bruce Sir David collect. of excise, Charles' close can.

Bruce Mrs, or Gruntsburgh, portsburgh

Bruce or Kinloch, Charles's close, canongate

Bruce Captain, Warriston's close

Bruce   Pore keeper, excise office

Bruce James saddler, brido-street

Bruce William, upholsterer, head of Dickson's close

Bruce Wm, iron factor Wardrop's court

Bruce and mier, cross causey

Bruce Alexander, advocate, hall stairs wynd

Bruce Mrs, canongate foot

Bruce Mrs, Leighton

Bruce Thomas, depute clerk of session, west bow foot

Bruce Alexander, merchant, west bow

Bruce John, writer, James' court

Bruce George, writer, west bow foot

Bruce Adam, writer, new assembly close

Bruce David, slater, Dunbar's close

Bruce Robert, slater, Stonelaw's close

Bruce Mrs, teacher of needle work, Brodie's close

Bruce Edward, writer, Forrester's wynd
Bruce George, Siennes
Bruce William, merchant, Brodie's close
Bruce Alexander, cabinet maker, &c Morison's close
Brunton Walter, saddler, op. head of blackfriars wy.
Brunton James, glass grinder, nether bow
Brunton John, merchant, head of Libberton's wynd
Brunton John, stay maker, bow-head with
Bryce, Thomas, hard-ware merchant, luckenbooths
Bryce George, grocer cowgate-head
Bryce Mrs, of Kello front of Adam's square
Bryce John, writer, Milo's court
Bryden James, shoe maker, canongate head
Bryson Robert, baker head of patterson's court
Bryson David, baker, Chrichton street
Bryson Thomas, brewer, siennes
Buchan-Hepburn George, advocate, James' cou t
Buchan John, writer to the signet, james' court
Buchan James, writer west-bow
Buchan John, jun. writer, James' court
Buchan John, 3tio, writer, cowgate head
Buchan William, physician, horse wynd
Buchan John, baxter, head of the pleasance
Buchan John, grocer, opposite Queensberry lodging
Buchan James, mason new street
Buchan Hugh, city chamberlin, front of exchange
Buchan Tho, of Auchmairne , advo. Shakespeare's sq,
Buchan George, Esq: of Kello, Adams' square
Buchan Mrs, James court
Buchan Francis, merchant, luckenbooths
Buchan William, accomptant, Goodwin's l. west-bow
Buchan George, advocate, Adam's square
Buchan Mrs, Boyd's close
Buchan   , high school wynd
Buchanan John, of Cairnmore, head of high school wy
Buchanan Mrs, Nicolson's street
Buchanan David, barber, foot of Bell's wynd
Buchanan John, shoe-maker, potter-row
Buchanan John, baker, head of St John's street
Buchanan John, confectioner, cowgate head
Buchie George, silk dyer, below canongate kirk
Buckney Mrs, St Mary's wynd

Buckney Andrew, shoe-maker, potter-row
Budge Mrs, potter-row
Burnside Mrs, room-setter, north Gray's close
Burnet Mrs, mantua maker, canongate-head
Burnet James, English teacher, grass market
Burnet William clerk to the exchequer, broughton
Burn William, leather merchant, Libberton's wynd
Burn Robert, merchant, head of Dickson's close
Burt John, shoe maker, hunters park
Burton George, hard-ware merchant, front of exchange
Burton George, wright castle bank
Burrel John, baker, pleasance
Burrel Andrew, shoe maker, canongate-head
Burrel Alexander, shoe-maker, op. linen hall, canongs
Butter and Son, wrights, Carruber's close
Butter John, merchant, lawn-market
Butter Mises, Carrubbers close
Butter Mrs, Carrubber's close
Butter John, book-binder, bow-head
Butter Mrs, Nicolson's street
Butcher William, feeds man, abbey-hill

C

Caddel John, stone-ware merchant, Dunbar's close
Cairncrofs George, writer, parliament square
Cairncrofs James, taylor, crofs causey
Cairnton John, brewer, head of the pleasance
Cairnton Robert, smith, Allan's close
Cairnmuir Lady, goose dub
Caitchen James, candle maker, candle maker row
Caitchen John, carver and gilder, foot of horse wy.
Caithness Mrs, St John's street
Caldwell Alex, vintner, op. foot of Peebles wynd
Caldwell John, portrait painter, Skinner's close
Calder John, grocer, grass market, north side
Calder Alexander, writer, exchequer fountain close
Calder Hugh, wright, pleasance
Calder James, grocer, west-bow
Callender John, advocate, St Andrew's square
Callender Geo. cabinet-maker and measurer, Scot's cl.
Callender John, clerk of session, head of Brodie's close
Callender Mrs, Libberton's wynd

Callender Mrs, room-setter, oppofite bridge-ftreet
Callender Mifs, mantu maker, cowgate head
Callender Mrs William, brifto-ftreet
Cameron George, engraver, &c. Tederick's wynd
Cameron Mrs, keeps boarders. brifto ftreet
Cameron Allan, meffenger, College wynd
Cameron James, taylor, Paterfon's court
Cameron John, merchant, lawn market, north fide
Cameron Archibald, painter, Miln's clofe, canongate
Cameron Hugh, upholfterer, canongate
Cameron Daniel, vintner. flefh market clofe
Cameron John, ftabler canongate head
Carmichael William, of Fairfield advo Carruber's clofe
Campbell Remonitone, fecretary. hope park
Campbell Mrs, of Aul, Shakefpeare fquare
Campbell Lady of Lochnel, Paterfon's court
Campbell Mrs, of Crinel, Shakefpeare fquare
Campbell Mrs, of Shuving, St Andrew's ftreet
Campbell John, of Ayrfhire, new-ftreet
Campbell Mrs head of St John's ftreet
Campbell Mifs, of Abrachill, Leith wynd
Campbell Robert, captain, St Mary's wynd
Campbell Lady Mary, Taylor's land canongate
Campbell Mrs, of South-hall, St Andrew's ftreet
Campbell Walter, advocate, Brown's fquare
Campbell Hay, advocate, fociety
Campbell Mrs Argyle's fquare
Campbell Robert colonel, Nicolfon's ftreet
Campbell Archibald, clerk of feffion, James' court
Campbell Mifs, of Bowerhill, Shakefpeare fquare
Campbell Duncan, writer, back ftairs
Campbell Colonel, of Phnab, Nicolfon's ftreet
Campbell Agnus, merchant, in the caftle-hill
Campbell John, grocer, Jock's land, canongate
Campbell John, fhoe maker, canongate foot
Campbell William, taylor, canal ftreet
Campbell John, grocer, foot of Merlin's wynd
Campbell Mrs, room letter, old affembly clofe
Campbell John, wright, Hammermen's clofe, cowg.
Campbell John, writer, Ramfay garden, caftle hill
Campbell Alexander, brewer, Rattray's clofe cowgate
Campbell John, fchool-mafter, fhoe-makers land can.

Campbell Alexander, grocer, or, meal market ſta'rs
Campbell James, merchant, cowgate-head
Campbell Mrs, Forreſier's wyd
Campbell Finlay, cooper, lawn market
Campbell John, ſtabler, canongate head
Campbell Samuel, book binder, weſt bow
Campbell Alexander, meſſenger, Toderick's wynd
Campbell George, wine-merchant, Campbell's cloſe
Campbell Thomas, merchant, oppoſite the guard
Campbell Mrs, Riddel's cloſe
Campbell William, ſchool-maſter, potter-row
Campbell Archibald, brewer, Campbell's cloſe cowg
Campbell James, ſhoe-maker, Toderick's wynd
Campbell John, writing man, below Halkerſton's wy.
Campbell Mrs, midwife, Arlie cloſe
Campbell Mrs, Shakeſpear's ſquare
Campbell Mrs, chapel ſtreet
Campbell Mungo, oppoſite Clibton's entry
Campbell Mrs, of Bly hfwood, Argyle's ſquare
Campbell Mrs, of Ballimore, St Andrew's ſquare
Campbell Mrs, room letter, old aſſembly cloſe
Campbell Thomas, ſociety
Campbell Peter, writer, new bank calton hil
Campbell Archibald, merchant, calton hill
Campbell William, writer to ſignet, St David's ſtreet
Campbell Mrs, of Tofts, new ſtreet
Campbell Mrs, room-letter, prince's ſtreet
Cantly Alexander, porter ſeller, head of Craig's cloſe
Carthae James, woolen draper, front of exchange
Cargill Andrew, cutler, Leith wynd
Cargill and Miller, iron-mongers, at the croſs
Cargill Daniel, cutler, Leith wynd
Carlyle Francis, writer, Shakeſpeare ſquare
Carmichael James, writer, Miln's court
Carmichael Andrew, writer, Shakeſpeare ſquare
Carmichael John, writer, Shakeſpeare ſquare
Carmichael Thomas, writer, Miln's court
Carmichael Thomas, merchant, front of Exchange
Carmichael John, wine-merchant, St Andrew's ſquare
Carmichael Mrs, Jack's cloſe canongate
Carmichael Mrs, Lurieſton
Carmichael Mrs, room ſetter, Leith wynd

Carmichael Daniel, paton-maker, creams
Carmichael James, writer to fignet, Buchan n's court
Carmichael James, grocer, grafs market S. fide
Carmichael James. writer, new ftreet
Carnegy George, of Northefk, Efq, St Andrew's ftr.
Carnegy James, of Findhaven, thiftle court
Carnegie Lady Mary, foot of Baxter's clofe cowgate
Carnochan William, grocer, St Andrew's ftreet
Carnochan   , grocer brifto ftreet
Carie Mrs, of Cavers, in brifto-ftreet
Caires Miis, of Nifbet, George's fquare
Carie Mrs, Panmure's clofe canongate
Carre Captain Robert, Hanover ftreet
Carfe Alexander, cutler, back of the fountain well
Carftairs John, furgeon, canongate-head
Carthrae Mrs, baker, canongate foot
Carthrae William, merchant, Bull's clofe
Carney   , phyfician, calton-hill
Caffels William, wright, pleafance
Catanach Mrs, room-fetter, new bank clofe
Caw John, affiftant fec of excife, Cheffels' court
Caw   , book-binder, Gosford's clofe
Cauvine Lewis, french teacher, bifhop's land
Cauvine Jofeph, writer, bifhops land
Cavins Andrew, merchant, Dickfon's clofe
Cay John, of Charleton-hall, Efq, Alifon's fquare
Chalmers John, wright, old affembly clofe
Chalmers William, writer, bow-head
Chalmers Patrick, advocate, cowgate-head
Chalmers Mrs, back ftairs
Chalmers Major John, Miln's court
Chalmers Roderick, white iron fmith, h. Libberton's w.
Chalmers Sir George, thiftle court
Chalmers Mrs, Weir's clofe, canongate
Chalmers Robert, writer, Adams' fquare
Chalmers George, merchant, covenant clofe
Chalmers Mrs, cowgate-head
Chalmers Thomas, fmith, potter-row
Chalmers John, extractor, St Andrew's ftreet
Chalmers William, furgeon, back ftairs
Chalmers Alexander, baxter, Nicolfon's ftreet
Chalmers Mrs, late of Weir, fociety port

Chalmers George, plumber, foot of the pleafance
Chalmers James, writer to the fignet Wardrop's court
Chancelor Mrs, of Shieldhil, Weir's land canongate
Chaplain Mrs, room fetter, taylors land canongate
Charteris Francis, jun. of Amisfield, St Andrew's ftr.
Charteris Samuel, follicitor of cuftoms, exchange
Chatterly Theophilus, candle maker row
Cheaps Mifs, of Roffie, Leith wynd
Cheap James, of Sauchie, Efq, prince's ftreet
Cheap William, linen-draper, Hyndford's clofe
Cheap Henry, of Roffey, Carrubbers clofe
Cheffor Robert, ftay-maker, St Mary's wynd
Chifholm William, merchant, cowgate-port
Chifholm Mr, oppofite the Linen hall canongate
Chifholm Mrs, head of Gray's clofe
Chriftie John, wright, weft bow
Chriftie John, Efq. St John's ftreet
Chriftie Peter, grocer, twopenny cuftom
Chriftie Mrs, water-gate
Chriftie William, book binder, new ftairs
Chriftie George, fhoe maker, Nicolfon's ftreet
Chriftie George, black fmith, head of the pleafance
Chriftie James, cork cutter, foot of college wynd
Chriftie James, grocer, back of the fountain well
Chriftie William, mafon, broughton
Chriftie William, new ftreet, canongate
Chriftie Mrs Leith wynd
Chirnfide Thomas, printer, Crichton's ftreet
Churchill Charles, captain, Nicolfon's fquare
Clapperton Mrs, merchant, luckenbooths
Clapperton James, lint dreffer, head of Scott's clofe
Clapperton George, writer, Byer's clofe
Clapperton Mrs, trunk clofe
Clark Alexander. writer, Monteith's clofe
Clark Captain John, at Mr Shaw's James court
Clark John, optician oppofite the guard
Clark James, glazier, Kinloch's clofe, canongate
Clark John, fhoe-maker, potter-row port
Clark George Maxwell, compt. of cuftoms, James' c.
Clark Mrs, caftle-hill
Clark Mrs, croft-angry
Clark James, kings ferrier, fouth back of canongate

Clark Robert, glazer, Toderick's wynd
Clark Robert, bookseller, kincaid's land cowgate
Clark Thomas and son, leather box manufact bristo-st
Clark Andrew, stay maker, portsburgh
Clark Mrs, room-letter, Adams' court
Clark John, of Eldin, head of west bow
Clark James, shoe-maker, exchange
Clark Duncan, tobacconist, front of Exchange
Clark James, grocer, opposite foot of Burnet's close
Clark Allan, writer to the signet, west bow foot
Clark Stephen, organist, blackfriars wynd
Clark David, writer, Mary kings close
Clark James, teacher of drawing, Wright's land, op-
    posite foot of Peebles wynd
Clark James, writer, opposite Crichton's entry can.
Clark Mrs, school-mistress cowgate head
Clark William, musician, Mortha's wynd
Clarkson James, baker, head of Swan's close
Clarkson William, hair-dresser, luckenbooths
Clarkson John, wine merchant canongate foot
Cleghorn Robert, student of divinity, Middleton's entry
Cleghorn Thomas, wright St Agnes street
Cleghorn Mrs, society port
Cleghorn Miss, Cleghorn's land grass-market
Cleghorn Misses, milliners, lucke booths
Cleghorn Thomas, wine-merchant, grass market
Cleghorn John, merchant, above Crichton's entry
Cleghorn Robert, gaoler, general's entry
Cleghorn Archibald, brewer, water of Leith
Cleghorn William, book binder, post house stairs
Cleghorn Miss, mantua maker, Middleton's entry
Cleland John, watch-maker, lawn market, N side
Cleland John, opposite foot of Niddery's wynd
Cleland Robert, jeweler, canongate head
Cleland Mrs, room-letter, Forrester's wynd
Cleland Miss, mantua-maker, canongate-head
Clephan James, wright, shoe-makers close, canongate
Clephan George of Carslogie, British linen hall
Cleugh John, hair-dresser, foot of the pleasance
Clidsdale Robert, clock-maker, back of the guard
Clidsdale Miss, mantua-maker, bunwermer's close
Clayton Thomas, plaisterer, Leith wynd

Cochrane Mrs, of Waterfide, bailie Fyfe's clofe

Cochrane, earl of Dundonald, St Ann's yards

Cochrane Thomas, fhoe-maker, head of the pleafance

Cock Charles, brewer, drumdry

Cock John, leather dreffer, Bell's mills

Cock Daniel, hair dreffer, foot of Niddery's wynd

Cockburn Archibald, fheriff depute, Brodie's clofe

Cockburn Mrs, blackfriars wynd

Cockburn Mrs, George's fquare

Cockburn Mrs, Monteith's clofe

Cockburn Robert, merc near Crichton's entry canon.

Cockburn John, english teacher, bailie Fyfe's clofe

Cockburn Thomas, ring's writer, Nicolfon's fquare

Cockburn Thomas, baxter, caufey fide

Cockburn Andrew, writer, Nicolfon's ftreet

Cockburn William, brewer, head of the pleafance

Cockburn James, cl to linen hall, Hunter's park

Cockburn Andrew, tin plate worker, bow head well.

Cockburn John, ftabler, brifto ftreet

Colftream John, writer in the commiffary office

Collare Mrs, carton hill

Colfton Lady, caftle-hill

Colquhoun George, yarn manufacturer, back row

Colquhoun Sir James, peebles wynd

Colquhoun-Grant James, advocate, Peebles wynd

Colquhoun Sir George, boneyhaugh

Colquhoun Archibald, vintner, Libberton's wynd

Colvill Lady, drumfheugh

Colvill Robert, wright, Nicolfon's ftreet

Colvill Lord, of Culrofs, St John's ftreet, canongate

Colvill Mifs, abbey ftrand

Colvin Mrs, cardle maker, abbey

Colzier Peter, conftable of excife, Campbell's clofe

Colzier Mifs, mantua-maker, campbell's clofe cowgate

Comb David, grocer, head of Patterfon's court

Combs George, brewer, Hamilton's folly

Combs Thomas, vintner, Shakefpeare fquare

Cooper George, teacher of mufic, back of exchange

Cooper and Bruce, hard ware merchants, luckenbooths

Cooper Mifs, Taylor's land canongate

Cooper David, ftabler, twopenny cuftom

Conney John, stucco plaisterer, Gabriel row
Congalton Mis, high school yards
Congalton Mises, canongate head
Constable George, writer, advocates close
Coomans John, teacher of languages, college wynd
Comb Mathew, baxter, Charles street
Cooper W. upholsterer, opposite Blackfriar's wynd
Cooper Archibald, grocer, foot of Peebles wynd
Copland William, advocate, new street
Copland James, book-binder, Henderson's stairs
Corbet John, taylor, St Mary's wynd
Corbet John, of Toll-crofs, Craig's close
Corbet Robert, advocate, candlemaker-row
Corrie Deminico, comely garden
Corrie Hugh, clerk to the signet, St Andrew's square
Cosnans Mis, Campbell's land, canongate
Cossar Walter, back of the meadows
Cossar David, stabler, two-penny custom
Cotton George, tobacconist, crofs cauley
Couden Hugh, baxter, Magdalen's chapel
Coulter William, hosier, facing the crofs well N. side
Coulter Mrs, stabler, grass market, north side
Coult Oliver, of Oldhame, opposite Queensberry lodg.
Coutts Alexander, taylor, Warriston's close
Coutts William, shoe-maker, Thomson's land canong.
Coutts Miss, Alison's square
Cowan John, engraver, covenant close head
Cowan William, founder, Niddery's wynd
Cowan William, merchant, bridge street
Cowan James, clock and watch-maker, parliament sq.
Cowan James, candle maker, opposite west bow
Craig Mrs, fountain close
Craig John, Gosfords close
Craig David, baker, Shakespeare square
Craig Thomas, of Riccarton, Carrubber's close
Craig William, advocate, meal-market stairs
Craig John, reed maker, castle wynd
Craig William, wright, Niddery's wynd
Craig James, architect, west bow foot
Craig Miss, mantua maker, horse wynd
Craig Robert, commissary, Carruber's close
Craigie John, advocate, Brown's square

Craig James, baxter, head of Kinloch's clofe
Craigie David, writer to the fignet, Brown's fquare
Craigie Thomas, taylor, canongate head, north fide
Craigie Thomas, ftay-maker, St Mary's wynd
Craigie Thomas, baker, abbey
Craigie William Charles, writer to the fignet, potter-r.
Craigie Lawrence, writer to the fignet, Alifon's fquare
Craigie George, fhoe-maker, pleafance
Cramb William, breeches maker, potter-row
Crammei William, mufician, Chalmers' clofe
Cranfton Mifs, Charles' ftreet
Cranfton James, fchool-mafter, Niddery's wynd
Craw William, faddler, back of the fountain well
Craw George, lockfmith, Dunbar's clofe canongate
Craw William, trockei, canongate church
Crawford Sii Hugh, red braes
Crawford James, writer to the fignet, Byers' clofe luck
Crawford William, fmith, middle of weft bow
Crawford John, ftabler, grafs market
Crawford Maurice and Co. copperfmiths. canongate-h.
Crawford Patrick of Auchenames, St Andrew's fquare
Crawford William, reed maker, Leith wynd
Crawford Alexander, baxter, foot of Bell's wynd
Crawford Peter, merchant, lauriefton
Crawford Mifs, canongate
Crawford Mifs, Brown's fquare
Crawford Mifs, chapel ftreet
Cree John, ftabler, foot of the pleafance
Creech William, bookfeller E. end of luckenbooths
Creech Alexander, ftay-maker, chapel-ftreet
Crichton Archibald, ftabler, grafs-market, fouth fide
Crichton James, mafon, Crichton ftreet
Crichton Mrs, new-ftreet
Crichton Alexander, coach-maker, canongate
Crichton James, brewer, N. back of the canongate
Crichton Lady, Penelope, Prefident's ftairs
Crooks Thomas, baker, grafs market north fide
Crooks Thomas, writer, weft bow
Crooks Mrs, Forrefter's wynd
Crofbie Andrew, advocate, St Andrew's fquare
Cruikfhanks George, writer, Borthwick's clofe

Cruickshanks W. master of high school, Kincaid's land
Crumbie Andrew, dyer, Hume's close
Culbert William, hair-dresser, h. of Halkerston's wy.
Culbertson Mrs, Charles street
Cullen William, physician, mint close
Cullen Robert, advocate, mint close
Cullen Mr, St Andrew's square
Cumming and Son, bankers, exchange
Cumming Alexander, spirit dealer, downm. baxters cl.
Cumming George, grocer, Morrocco's land canongate
Cumming James, painter, new street
Cumming William, shoe-maker, w. end of Lauriston
Cumming Miss mantua maker, west bow
Cumming James, late of Brado, Nicolson's street
Cumming John, writer, high school yards
Cumming John, messenger, anchor close, scale stairs
Cumming Robert, ship master, fish market close
Cumming George, writer, at Mr Wauchope's horse wy.
Cumming George, lint dresser, opposite Chessels' court
Cumming Robert, stay-maker, foot of cross causey
Cumming Thomas, flesher, bull's close
Cumming Charles, baxter grass market
Cumming Mrs chapel street
Cumming Robert, professor, Charles street
Cumming and Hall, milliners, luckenbooths
Cumming Mrs, room setter, old excise office
Cunningham Alex. writer to the signet, old bank close
Cunningham Mrs, Nicolson's street
Cunningham Mrs, Chessels' court
Cunningham Mrs, of Campblebank, Charles' street
Cunningham Alex 3?..s, writer, new assembly close
Cunningham Mrs, baxter, grass-market south side
Cunningham David, baxter, west bow foot
Cunningham Alexander, writer, Grant's close west-bow
Cunningham John, mason, Peebles wynd
Cunningham James, jun. baxter, head of Burnet's close
Cunningham Mrs, chapel street
Cunningham Miss, chapel street
Cunningham W. and P gold smiths castle hill
Cunningham James, sen baxter, h. of blackfriars wy.
Cunningham ward, writer, Barrenger's close
Cunningham Alexander, corn merchant, fountain br.

Cunningham Thomas, dyer, fountain bridge

Currie George, advocate fountain close

Currie Mifs, mantua maker, Blackfriars wynd

Currie Mifs, milliner, back of the fountain well

Currie James, of Crile, Stodarts close cowgate

Currie Mrs, bunker's hill

Cuthbert Abner, at major Johnston's, Nicolfon's ftreet

Cuthbert Thomas, captain, croft angry

Cuthbertfon William, ladler, back of the guard

D

Dalgliefh George, wright, Middleton's entry

Dalgliefh Hugh, room-letter, canongate-head

Dalgliefh James, writer Brown's clofe, luckenbooths

Dalgliefh and Mathie, watch makers, and jewelers, parliament fquare

Dalgliefh James, clerk and auctioneer, potter-row

Dalgliefh James, grocer, head of the old bank clofe

Dalgliefh Robert, druggift, head of the pleafance

Dallas Alex. fen. of North Newton, blackfriars wynd

Dallas George, writer to the fignet, Niddery's wynd

Dallas Henry, fhoe maker St Ninian's row

Dallas Mrs, caftle-hill

Dallas William, wright, foot of the anchor clofe

Dallas Mifs crofs caufey

Dallas Mrs, calton hill

Dalle James, officer of excife, fiennes

Dalling Robert, examiner of excife, Campbell's clofe

Dallaway William, japanner, below canongate church

Dalmahoy John, fhoe & harnefs ware houfe Jack's l. can

Dalrymple William, merchant, prince's ftreet

Dalrymple Hugh, captain, end of potter-row

Dalrymple Sir John, Nicolfon's fquare

Dalrymple Lady Dowager, chapel ftreet

Dalrymple John, Efq, Queen's ftreet

Dalrymple Lady, of Caftleton, chapel ftreet

Dalrymple George, vintner, prefident ftairs

Dalrymple Mrs, of Harrifon, Charles ftreet

Dalziel Mrs, college wynd

Dalziel Profeffor college wynd

Darling William, printer, advocates clofe

Darling William, fhoe-maker, crofs-caufey

Darling John, fhoe-maker, potter-row

Darling Robert, mathematician, opposite the guard
Davidson John, writer to the signet, castle-hill
Davidson Mrs, Pirrie's close canongate
Davidson Daniel, painter, bow-head
Davidson John Exchequer
Davidson Adam, permit exam. Nicolson's street
Davidson Francis, taylor, castle-hill
Davidson Robert, writer, M'Kenzie's office
Davidson Mrs, room-setter, Baron Maule's close
Davidson Mrs, room-setter, upper common close
Davidson Mrs, of Kattree, grass market
Davidson Robert, brewer, canongate foot
Davidson Robert, shoe-maker, above the crackling h.
Davidson Thomas, lint dresser, blackfriars wynd
Davidson William, writer, Cooper's land canongate
Davidson William, wig-maker head of Chalmers close
Davidson William, school maker, north back of can.
Davidson William cooper, foot of Libberton's wynd
Davidson of Restalrig, society.
Davidson and Porteous, smiths, pleasance
Davidson, of white house, new town
Davidson Mrs, chapel street.
Davie Adam, deacon of Goldsmiths, Henderson's stairs
Davie Mrs smith potter-row
Davie John, Esq; Nicolson's street
Davie Thomas, tobacconist, portsburgh
Davie William, jeweler, west entry to parliament sq.
Dawson John, founder, portsburgh
Dawson William, merchant, Gladstone's land, lawn m.
Dean Peter, wright, Nicolson's street
Deans Alexander, wright, Middleton's entry
Deans James, stocking-needle maker potter-row
Deas William, silk-dyer, opposite the weigh house
Deas William, dyer, portsburgh
Deas William painter, St Mary's wynd
Dempster William, jeweler, parliament square
Dempster John, grocer, head of Kinloch's close
Denham David, shoe-maker, St Ninian's row
Denham John, baxter, bow head
Denham Mrs, Skiners close
Denholm Robert, writer, at J. Wemyss, silk dyer, cow
Denovan Campbell, printer, Turk's close lawn market

Descury Captain, prince's street
Dewhar David, seal cutter, parliament square
Dewar Mrs, of Vogrie, Libberton's wynd
Dewars Miss, Chrichton's street
Dewar Robert, glazier, Forrester's wynd
Dewar James of Vogrie, horse wynd
Dewar Mrs, castle wynd
Dewar George, linen draper, luckenbooths
Dewar James, merchant, opposite bridge street.
Dick Alexander, vintner, old post house close
Dick David, brewer, foot of college wynd
Dick Thomas, vintner head of Gray's close
Dick John, barber, opposite canongate church
Dick Robert, professor, Alison's square
Dick Rober, writer, broughton
Dick William, merchant, grass-market
Dickie Matthew, writer, Miln's court
Dickie Alexander, watch maker, bridge street
Dickie Mrs, St Andrew's street
Dickie William, writer, calton hill
Dickieson Alexander, glazier, St Andrew's square
Dickson Miss, mantua-maker, Morrocco's close canon.
Dickson James, bookseller, front of exchange
Dickson John, advocate, back stairs
Dickson William, advocate, Burnet's close
Dickson James, smith, Nicolson's street
Dickson John, wright, Nicolson's street
Dickson Mrs, of Hartree, Murdoch's close
Dickson Miss, Kincaid's land, cowgate
Dickson Mrs, Charles' street
Dickson Thomas, mason, abbey-hill
Dickson William, wright, below canongate church
Dickson Miss, Milliner, Forrester's wynd
Dickson Mrs of Carberry head of flesh market close
Dingwall John, writer, sheriff clerk's office, lawn m.
Dingwall Alexander, grocer, front of James' court
Dobie George, mason, Nicolson's street
Dobson William, baker, cross causey
Domvile Henry, linen ware room canongate
Donald Robert, writer, nether-bow
Donald James, druggist, opposite the guard
Donaldson David, wright and glazier, calton hill

Donaldſon Robert, writer to the ſignet, prince's ſtreet
Donaldſon James, carver and guilder, Magdalden chap
Donaldſon James, printer and bookſeller, at the croſs
Donaldſon Nathaniel, writer, Baxter's land graſs m.
Donaldſon Mrs, of Brownhills, Aliſon's ſquare
Donaldſon John, painter, foot of horſe wynd
Donaldſon Thomas, confectioner, Leith wynd
Donaldſon Mrs, foot of new ſtreet
Donaldſon Mrs, candle maker foot of Gabriel's road
Dorret William, ſmith, Nicolſon's ſtreet
Dott Robert, reed-maker, caſtle wynd
Dougall James, hair-dreſſer, nether bow
Dougall Joſeph, wright, Nicolſon's ſtreet
Douglas Mrs, of Tileculy, Hanover-ſtreet
Douglas Andrew, glazier, Forreſter's wynd
Douglas Daniel, vintner, advocate's cloſe
Douglas Lady, Ramſay garden caſtle-hill
Douglas John, ſword-ſlipper, canongate foot
Douglas John, hatter, Monteith's cloſe
Douglas Mrs, of Glenbervy, St John's ſtreet
Douglas Mrs, Nicolſon's ſtreet
Douglas Mrs, of Finglaſſie, New ſtreet
Douglas Robert, ſhoe-maker, cauſey ſide
Douglas Walter, ſhoe-maker, St Ninian's row
Douglaſ Miſs, milliners ſouth Gray's cloſe
Douglas Andrew, taylor, foot of old fiſh market cloſe
Douglas Robert, paper-maker, op. old fiſh mark. cloſe
Douglas Mrs, of Cavers, George's ſquare
Douglas   , oppoſite Queenſberry lodging
Douglas Robert, Campbell's land, canongate
Douglas George, Eſq; Aitken's laud canongate
Douglas George, writer, back of exchange
Douglas Mrs, Shakeſpear's ſquare
Douglas Lillias, milliner, oppoſite the guard
Dow David, wright, Bell's wynd
Dow John, grocer, oppoſite the meal market ſtairs
Dow John, cork cutter, op foot of Libberton's wynd
Dow Peter, hoſier, head of Toderick's wynd
Dow Daniel, muſician, Toderick's wynd
Dow Miſs, mantua-maker, upper baxters cloſe
Dow Mrs, St Mary's wynd
Dowie John, vintner, Libberton's wynd

Dowie Charles, baker, end of the crofs caufey
Dowie Adam, land furveyor, loch-rin
Downie Mrs, mantua-maker, caftle-hill
Downie Mrs, room-fetter, Carruber's clofe
Downie Walter, fhoe maker, above the crackling houfe
Downie D. goldfmith, parliament fquare
Drummond Mrs. blackfriars wynd
Drummond Captain, Strichan's clofe
Drummond Mrs, at the tron church
Drummond Honrable Mrs, caftle hill
Drummond Mrs, keeps boarders, Carruber's clofe
Drummond, bookfeller, Offian's head at the crofs
Drummond Alexander, French teacher, Craig's clofe
Drummond William, grocer, head of Toderick's wynd
Drummond Mrs, brifto-ftreet
Drummond Lewis, captain, Warrifton's clofe
Drummond Grigor, flefher, flefh-market clofe
Dryfdale Alexander, copper fmith, weft bow
Dryfdale William, ftabler, head of horfe wynd
Dryfdale John, minifter, Shakefpear's fquare
Dryfdales Mifs, milliners, flefh market clofe
Dudgeon Alexander, glazier, potter-row
Dudgeon Robert, baker, foot of Cant's clofe
Duff John, room-fetter, flefh-market clofe
Duff Lauchlane, writer to the fignet, James's court
Duff Mis, Cant's clofe
Duff Lady Ann, George's fquare
Duffes Charles, writer, bunkers hill
Dumbreck John, vintner, Miln's fquare
Dun James, wright, weft end of laurifton
Dun James, Hotel, prince's ftreet, new town.
Dunbar William, ftabler, grafs market
Dunbar Sir James, new ftreet
Dunbar Mrs, Don's clofe
Dunbar Mrs, Mochrum, Cheffels building
Dunbar William, writer to the fignet, oppo. the guard
Dunbar Mrs, boarder, Adam's court
Dunbar George, merchant and mafon, calton hill
Dunbar Mifs, Forrefter's wynd
Dunbar Mrs, vintner, Libberton's wynd
Dunbar Keith, writer to the fignet, Chrichton ftreet
Dunbar James, merchant, lawn marker, north fide

Dunbar William, weaver, hammerman's clofe canon.
Duncan Henry, merc. filk & wool dyer, luckenbooths
Duncan George, comptroller of ftamps, ftamp office
Duncan Alex. writer to the fignet, St Andrew's ftreet
Duncan James, vintner, Byers' clofe
Duncan Andrew, phyfician, brifto-ftreet
Duncan James, taylor, Hunter's park
Duncan James, baker portfburgh
Duncan John, fchool-mafter, canongate head
Duncan William, merchant, grafs market, fouth fide
Duncan George, comptroller of excife, fountain clofe
Duncan John, meal maker, meal market
Duncan John Libberton's wynd
Duncan Mis, Gentles clofe, canongate
Dundas Henry, lord advocate, George's fquare
Dundas Doctor, teviot-row
Dundas Mrs Helen, Turk's clofe
Dundas John, writer to the fignet, head of college wy
Dundas Lawrence, keeper of the excife, Cheffels' court
Dundas Thomas, advocate, St Andrew's fquare
Dundaffes Mifs, milliners, head of Don's clofe
Dundas Mifs, new ftreet
Dundas Mrs, wind-miln ftreet
Dundas Ralph, Alifon's fquare
Dundas Mrs, Leith wynd
Dundas Mifs, merlin's wynd
Dundas Mrs, weft bow
Dunkinfon Mrs, of Kello, Nicolfon's ftreet
Dunfmuir John, and George, merchants luckenbooths
Dunfmuir John, fchool-matter, baillie Fyfe's clofe
Dupafquier Leonard, carver and gilder St Agnes ftreet
Dupont Peter, minifter, oppofite Magdalden's chapel
Durham James, Efq; George's fquare
Durham Alexander, grocer, caftle hill
Durward Jofeph, watch maker, head of new ftreet
Duvall Alexander, grocer, head of the covenant clofe

E

Eagle Mrs, merchant, below baillie Fyfe's clofe
Eafton Mrs, grocer, canongate
Eafton John, procurator, Allan's clofe
Eafton John, grocer, portfburgh
Eccles Martin, phyfician, George's fquare

Edgar John, writer to the fignet, horfe wynd,
Edgar James, vintner, old poft houfe clofe
Edgar John, writer in the excife, Leith wynd
Edmond David, goldfmith, calton
Edmondfton Governor, Reid's court, canongate
Edmondfton Mrs, plainftone clofe canongate
Edmondfton Ifaac, ftabler, cowgate port
Edmondfton James, writer, Amisfeld
Edmondfton Mrs, milliner, Leith wynd
Edwards Alex. of Eaft India comp. old affembly clofe
Elder Thomas, wine merchant, Prince's ftreet
Elder James, ftabler, two penny cuftom
Elliot Cornelius, writer to the fig. St Andrew's fquare
Elliot Charles, bookfeller, parliament fquare, houfe
   above Walker's tavern writer's court
Elliot Mrs, midewife, Dickfon's clofe
Eliot Jofeph, painter and colourman Nether bow
Elliot John, britifh coffee houfe, generals entry
Elliot Jofeph, barber, canongate head
Elliot Mrs, fountain well
Elliot Mrs, Carruber's clofe
Elliots Mifs, milliners, Dickfon's clofe
Elliot Mifs, mantua-maker, Dickfon's clofe
Elliot Sir Francis, back of the meadow
Elliot Mifs, Brown's fquare
Elphingfton Alexander, advocate, Carruber's clofe
Elphingfton Lord Charles, kirk-brae-head
Englifh Mifs, milliner, bridge-ftreet
Emflie John, writer, Libberton's wynd
Erfkine The Honourable Henry, advocate George's fq
Erfkine The Honourable Andrew, Drumfheugh
Erfkine Charles, Efq. Semple's clofe, caftle-hill
Erfkine Mrs, of Balgowry, oppo. Queenfberry lodging
Erfkine Lady Charlotte, Gayfield
Erfkine Mrs, Semple's clofe
Erfkine John, minifter, laurifton
Erfkine Mifs, Campbell's clofe cowgate
Erfkine David, writer to the fignet, Argyle's fquare
Erfkine, of Cardrofs, horfe wynd
Efplin Robert, brewer, grafs market fouth fide
Efplin Charles, and Co. paper ftainers, h. of Swan's Us

Esplin Michael, shoe maker, Thomson's land cowgate
Eslope Mrs, back stairs
Espy William, distiller, head of Lady Stairs close
Ewart Thomas, copper smith, Leith wynd
Ewart Mifs, merchant, luckenbooths
Ewart Thomas, stabler, candle maker row
Ewing Alex teacher of mathematics, Bishop's land
Ewing James, writer, St Andrew's street

F

Fairbairn Mrs, room-setter, opposite the weigh house
Fairbairn George, baker, lawn market
Fairnbairn John, book binder, back of the weigh house
Fairbairn James, baxter, pleasance
Fairholme of Greenlaw, Ramsay garden, castle hill
Fairholme Thomas, merchant Blyth's close castle-hill
Fairholme James, wig-maker, h. of old assembly close
Fairweather David, feeds man, pleasance
Fairweather Mifs, portsburgh
Falconer David, advocate, Chalmers's close
Falconer George, of Carlowrie, Foulis' close
Falconer David, clerk to the weigh house
Falconer James, of Monkton, Esq ; Miln's square
Falconer The right reverend William, fountain close
Falls Mifs, Nicolson's street
Fall Mifs, Weir's close, canongate
Farnie John, baker, fountain close
Farm Mifs opposite, bow head well
Farm James, hair dresser, head of Morrison's close
Farquhar Alex. stabler cowgate head
Farquhar James, merc. W. end of St Andrew's square
Farquharson Peter, grocer, head of Morison's close
Farquharson David, glover, nether bow
Farquharson Alexander, writing master, Grant's close
Farquharson Alexander, accomptant, Adam's square
Farquharson Henry, carver and gilder St Mary's wy.
Farquharson Mrs, grocer, front of Cheffels' court .
Farquharson Mrs, Craig's close
Farquharson Mrs, room-setter, canongate head
Farquharson Mrs, room-setter Foulis' close
Fawer Mrs, mantua-maker, Bishop's land
Fawcit Samuel Bishop's land
Fell Thomas, grocer, head of Cant's close

Fenton John, painter, at the crackling house
Fenton Mrs, Hyndford's close
Fenton William, brewer, water-gate
Fenwick William, cooper, St Ninian's row
Fergus Mrs, keeps boarders, Chalmers' close
Fergus Mrs, Strichan's close
Ferguson Neil, advocate, post office stairs
Ferguson James, copper smith, grafs market
Ferguson Alex. of Craigdarroch, Esq. St Andrew str.
Ferguson John, grocer, St Mary's wynd
Ferguson Adam, prof. of moral philof. Nicolfon's str.
Ferguson George, advocate, back stairs
Ferguson James of Pitfour, advocate, luckenbooths
Ferguson James, writer, Bishop's land
Ferguson John, copper-smith well bow
Ferguson Mifs lawn-market, north side
Ferguson M. s, midwife, Craig's close
Ferguson Mrs, Shakefpeare fquare
Ferguson Robert, writer, foot of Forrefter's wynd
Ferguson Walter, writer, Gavinloch's land, lawn m.
Ferguson Walter, candle maker, lawn market
Ferguson Mungo, merchant, Henderfon's stairs
Ferguson Alexander, writer, Dickfon's close
Ferguson Alexander, dyer, west bow
Ferguson William, teacher, of lang. foot of Cant's close
Ferguson Alexander, foot of new stairs
Ferrie James, candle maker, abbey strand
Ferrie Mrs, soap boiler, Melvill's close canongate
Ferrier James, writer to the signet, Lady Stair's close
Ferrier James, farmer, grange mains
Ferrier John officer of excile, canongate foot
Fettes William, grocer, head of baillie Fyfe's close
Figgans James, writer, Borthwick's close
Fife Thomas, taylor, canongate
Finch Mrs, confectioner, corner of bridge street
Finlay Mrs, room-fetter, fountain close
Finlay John, stay maker, bull turnpike
Finlay David, wig maker, front of James' court
Finlay William, diftiller, croft angery
Finlayfon William, writer, Cant's close
Finlay John, hair dreffer, op. bow head well

Fisher John, engraver, luckenbooths
Fisher Andrew, grocer, head of old fish market
Fisher James, west bow
Fisher Mrs, room setter, upper baxters close lawn m
Fitch Alexander, book-binder, Forrester's wynd
Fitzsimons William revenue, bunker's hill
Fleming Mrs, baud close
Fleming Robert, printer, old fish market
Fletcher Archibald, writer, anchor close
Fletcher M s, room-setter, front of Paterson's court
Fletcher John, ginger bread baker, cross causey
Flockhart John, writer, newington
Foggo James, writer, Monteith's close
Foggo Mrs, Lockhart's close
Forbes Sir W. Hunter and Co. bankers, parliament sq.
Forbes William, er, city clerks chamber
Forbes Alexander, writer, bailie Fyfe's close
Forbes Duncan, blue and starch manuf, s side graf mar.
Forbes James, lint dresser, fish market close
        Lady, new-town
        Lady, Gray's close
        Mrs, new town
        Alexander, writer, to the signet, new street
        Mrs, mantua maker, bridge street
        illiam, Skiner's close
        David writer, lauriston
        Daniel, grocer, nether bow
        George, writer, Paul's work
        Robert, iron monger, head of Geddes' close
        dyce Mrs, thistle court
Fordyce John, general receiver, St Andrew's square
Forrest Andrew, merchant, Nicolson's street
Forrest Andrew, keeps boarders, cross
Forrest James, smith, cross causey
Forest James, of Comiston, bristo street
Forrest James, writer to the signet w, entry James' c.
Forrest John, jun. Miln's court
Forrest and Maxwell, wine merchants, Miln's court
Forrest Robert uphollt. and auctioneer, Chalmers close
Forrest William, grocer, west bow
Forrest William printer, foot of west bow
Forrest George, brewer, pleasance

Forreſt George, wig maker, op. the mint
Forreſter David, of Lanerk, Eſq. St Andrew's ſtreet
Forreſter Robert, of Cormiſton, George's ſquare
Forreſter P. jeweller and hard ware merc at the croſs
Forreſter William, ſilk manufacturer Leith wynd
Forreſter William, taylor, Nicolſon's ſtreet
Forreſter Mrs, weſt bow foot
Forſyth James, ſhoe-maker calton
Forſyth John, writer Niddrey's wynd
Forſyth James, book-binder, op. meal market ſtairs
Fortune John, vintner, oppoſite the guard
Fortune George, baker, Nicolſon's ſtreet
Fotheringham Kid, writer, Young's ſtreet
Fotheringham Oſwald, writer, downmoſt baxter's cl.
Fotheringham Mrs, Hyndford's cloſe
Fotheringham Fredrick, writer, bunkers hill
Fotheringham Miſs, Fiſher's cloſe
Foulis Mrs of Ratho, chapel ſtreet
Forwalt Chriſtopher, merchant op. canongate church
Fowler James, merchant, Nicolſon's ſtreet
Foy James, writing maſter, Skinne.'s cloſe
Fraſer Alexander, meſſenger, head of advocates cloſe
Fraſer Alexander, writer & meſſenger, Stevenlaw cl.
Fraſer James, writer, Currie's cloſe
Fraſer James, writer to the ſignet, St David's ſtreet
Fraſer Charles, buckram maker, at benny-haugh
Fraſer John writer to the ſignet, Mila's court
Fraſer Alex. clerk in the exciſe-office, canongate-head
Fraſer Simon, advocate, Nicolſon's ſtreet
Fraſer Mrs, vintner, parliament ſtairs
Fraſer William, white-iron-ſmith, Shakeſpear's ſquare
Fraſer Mrs, new ſtreet
Fraſer John, tanner, canongate foot
Fraſer John, white-iron-ſmith, weſt bow
Fraſer George, goldſmith, entry to Nicolſon's ſtreet
Fraſer James, clerk to the bakers, water of Leith
Fraſer John, wright, at the crackling houſe
Fraſer Simon, writer to the ſignet, Chrichton ſtreet
Fraſer Simon, captain of the tolbooth, weſt bow
Fraſer Luke, one of the high ſchool-maſters, Hay's
    court, potter-row
Fraſer Roderick, grocer, foot of Forreſter's wynd

Frafer James, writer in the bank, calton hill
Frafer Alexander, fen. writer, up. baxters clofe
Frafer Mrs, room fetter, flefh market clofe
French James, one of the high fchoolmafters, brifto-ftr.
French Samuel, clerk in the poft office, brifto ftreet
French Mrs, Stonelaw's clofe
Freebairn Mifs, boarding fchool, fociety
Freebairn David, merchant, back of bow head well
Friar Mifs, nether bow
Friar Mrs, potter-row
Frigge Alexander, tobacconift, brifto ftreet
Frigge David, writer chapel ftreet
Fryer George, tobacconift, old excife office
Fullerton Mifs, old play houfe clofe, canongate
Fullerton George, Efq. broughton hall
Fullerton William, Efq of Caftairs Nicolfon's ftreet
Fullwood John, grocer, Buccleugh ftreet
Fulton Thomas, fmith, potter-row
Fulton George, fchool mafter, Peebles wynd
Fyers Thomas, Efq, George's fquare
Fyfe James, fenr. merchant, luckenbooths
Fyfe John, banker, Wardrop's court
Fyfe Thomas, merchant grafs market

G

Gairdner Alexander, goldfmith, parliament fquare
Gairdner Alexander, feffion clerk, portfburgh
Gairdner Andrew, merchant, weft-port vennel
Gairdner Mifs, merchant, luckenbooths
Gairdner Ebenezer, linen manufacturer, portfburgh
Gairdner Humpry, Campbell's clofe, canongate
Gairdner George, brewer, goofe dub
Gairdner James, ferrier, candle-maker-row
Gairdner John, pewterer, nether bow
Gairdner Lawrence, wig maker, op. the old ex. cowg.
Gairdners C. & M, merchants luckenbooths
Gairdner Mrs, dyer, Scot's clofe, cowgate
Gairdner Richard, comp. old play-houfe clofe
Gairdner Mrs, vintner, cowgate port
Gairdner John phyfician, Niddrey's wynd
Gairdner William, fhoe-maker, weft bow
Gairdner Alexander, fmith and ferrier, cowgate port
Gairdner Mifs grafs market

Gairdner John, baxter, pleasance

Galbraith and Wallace, grocers head of Paterson's court

Galbraith Henry, printer, west bow

Galbraith Philip, smith, foot of the pleasance

Gall William, shoe-maker, portsburgh

Gall John hair-dresser cowgate

Galloway John, merchant, first sta. above tron church

Galloway William, merchant, luckenbooths

Galloway Mrs, flesh market close canongate

Garioch Alex. cl. to Sir William Forbes, James's court

Gartshore Mrs, Gosfords close

Garvie Mrs, room-setter, Shakespear's square

Gascoigne Mrs Cnarteris's close, canongate

Gavin Hector, engraver, parliament square

Gavin Joseph, grocer, main point

Gavin David compounder, main point

Gay John, hair-dresser, opposite the guard

Gay Thomas, hair-dresser, Wright's close cowgate

Ged Mrs, Paterson's court

Ged Robert, dyer, op. the foot of Stonelaw's close

Geddes James, grocer, cowgate head

Geddes James, wine-merchant, anchor-close

Geddes Mrs, bow head

Giekie John, barber, above the crackling house

Gentle James, brewer, Gentle's close

Gibb Adam, minister, Nicolson's street

Gibb James, grocer, opposite the linen hall

Gibb John, confectioner, Leith wynd

Gibb William, bookseller, parliament house

Gibb Andrew, potter-row port

Gibb Mrs, Young's street

Gib Mrs, room-setter, Miles land, canongate

Gib Mrs, boards gentlemen, East turnpike meal mar.

Gibson Daniel, smith, cross causey

Gibson John, wright, water-gate

Gibson William, taylor potter-row

Gibson Miss, grocer, bow-head

Gibson Mrs, stabler, grass market

Gibson of Cliftonhall, Esq; castle hill

Gibson John, watch maker, west end of luckenbooth

Gibson Mrs, castle hill

Gibson Lady, opposite linen hall canongate

Gibson William, merchant, bridge street
Gibson Peter, wright, cross causey
Gibson & Balfour, bankers, Buchanan's court
Gibson Thomas, clerk of session, Strichen's close
Gibson William, minister, at the west church
Gibson James, surgeon, opposite foot of Niddry's wynd
Gibson James, brewer, abbey
Gibson Charles, taylor, grass market
Gibson and Marr, smiths pleasance
Gibson Durie advocate, Chalmers close
Gibson Mrs flesh-market close
Gilbert James, brewer, north back of the canongate
Gilchrist John, grocer, cross causey
Gilchrist Mrs, mid-wife, college wynd
Gilchrist Peter, officer of excise, canon'mills brae head
Gilchrist Archibald, merchant, back of the guard
Gilchrist James stabler, Gullon's close canongate
Gilchrist Mrs, room setter, Carruber's close
Gifford Adam, leather-case-maker, cross causey
Giles Arthur, wright, college wynd
Gilles William, messenger, city clerk's office
Gilles Alexander, writer, tiend office calton hill
Gilles Henry, baker, canongate head
Gilles John, retailer, cowgate head
Gilles Miss, merchant, luckenbooths
Gillespie Andrew, upholsterer, clamshell turnpike
Gillespie James, tobacconist, opposite the guard
Gillespie John, fountain bridge
Gillespie and Fyfe, merchants, luckenbooths
Gillespie Mrs, Charles street
Gillespie James, writer, M'Kenzie's office, potter-row
Gillespie Mrs, Lochend's close canongate
Gilliland James, jeweller, parliament square
Gilkie James, writer, and notary, foot of Merlin's wynd
Gilmore Samuel, rope-maker, grass market
Gilmore Peter, rope-maker, west-port vennal
Gilmore John, Roperie, west bow
Gilmore Peter, goldsmith,
Gilmore Mrs, room setter, forrester's wynd
Gillon Mrs of Walhouse, St Andrew's street
Gives Anthony, blanket manufacturer, castle barns

Glasgow Lady, abbey
Glass Miss, Jack's land canongate
Glass Miss, mantua-maker, opposite meal market
Glen Thomas, physician, Herriot's bridge
Glenorchie Lady, St Andrew's street
Gloag John, merchant, luckenbooths
Gloag Mrs, Allison's square
Gloag William, minister. castle-hill
Glover John, white-iron-smith, luckenbooths
Gordon the Hon. Alexander, advocate, castle hill
Gordon Alexander, 3tio, advocate, Queen's street
Gordon Alexander, writer, Paterson's court
Gordon John, jun. writer to the signet, Adam's square
Gordon Charles, writer to the signet, George's square
Gordon John, senr. writer to the signet, Hanover sq.
Gordon James, Major, of Allen, Allen's close
Gordon Mrs, of Clunie, Seller's close lawn market
Gordon John, carver and gilder, canongate
Gordon James, brewer, grass market
Gordon Mrs, back of the guard
Gordon George, colonel, Reid's close canongate
Gordon James, accomptant to british linen hall canon.
Gordon Robert, Allison's square
Gordon James, accomptant, Dickson's close
Gordon John oyster seller, foot of Niddery's wynd
Gordon Mrs Hamilton, St Andrew's street
Gordon John, auctioneer, Dickson's close
Gordon William, bookseller, parliament square
Gordon Mrs, Nicolson's street
Gordon Robert, wright; goose dub
Gordon George, wr Mrs Maxwell's, Paterson's cout
Gordon John, vintner, Bess wynd
Gordon Robert, baker, head of St Mary's wynd
Gordon Mrs, lets rooms, foot of Forrester's wynd
Gordon Miss, mantua-maker, west bow
Gordon Archibald, cooper, twopenny custom
Gordon William, brewer, grass market
Good Andrew, wright, college wynd
Goodwin James, lint merchant, west bow
Goodsman James, hosier, h. of Libberton's wynd
Goodwillie John, closet keeper, Dalrymple's office

F

Goldie & Robertson, hard ware-merchants at the cross

Goldie George, merchant, british linen-hall

Goarley Oliver, writer, Skinner's close

Govan William, glazier, opposite the bow head well

Govan Alexander architect, St John's street

Gow Peter, schoolmaster, Forrester's wynd

Gow John, wright, castle hill

Gow John, shoe maker, pleasance head

Gowan Mrs, St John's street

Græme David, advocate, post house stairs

Graham William, Esq, of Airth, head of college wynd

Graham David, merchant, grass market

Graham Mrs, wool merchant, castle hill

Graham Mrs, keeps boarders Carruber's close

Graham John, writer to the signet, Gosford's close

Graham James, wright near the crackling house

Graham William, saddler Herriot's bridge

Graham John, advocate, bailie Fyfe's close

Graham Mr. of Gartmore, prince's street

Graham Mr . . . . wynd

Graham . . . . . late brewer, Gavinloch's land

Graham James clerk to the Glasgow waggon, grass m

Graham Andrew, late from Hudson's bay, chaple street,

Grandison Miles, milliners Leith wynd

Granger Mrs calton hill

Grant Mrs, James's court

Grant William, wire hive maker, castle hill

Grant James of Corrimoney, advocate anchor close

Grant Lady of Ballandalloch, Reid's close canongate

Grant Robert fish rod maker, back of the fountain well

Grant John writer, trustees office

Grant Gregory, physician, James's court

Grant Alexander sen writer, Morrocco's close lawn m

Grant Lewis, merchant opposite Forrester's wynd

Grant Colquhoun, writer to the signet, Gavinloch's land

Grant Alexander, merchant, Blackfriar's wynd

Grant Robert writer to the signet, Carruber's close

Grant Mrs of Prestongrange, St John's street

Grant James, merchant west bow

Grant Thomas, fishing rod maker, nether bow

Grant Alexander, jun taylor, mint close

Grant Alexander, fen. taylor, blackfriars wynd
Grant William, taylor, Niddery's wynd
Grant Ludovick, jun. writer, thiftle court
Grant Sir James, Bart. op. Queenfberry lodging can.
Grant Ilaac, writer to the fignet, Brown's fquare
Grant Ludovick fen. writer, St Andrew's fquare
Grant Archibald, captain, horfe wynd
Grant Alexander, writer, Niddrey's wynd
Grant William advocate, St Andrew's fquare
Grant John, fen. caftle-hill
Grant Robert, grocer, potter-row
Grant Mrs, foot of canongate
Grant William, retailer of fpirits, op. blackfriars wy.
Grant John, potterrow port.
Grant Mrs, George fquare
Grant Mifs, of Grant, opp Queenfberry lodging
Grant Mils, baillie Fyfe's clofe
Gray John, room fetter, Gosfords clofe
Gray James, ftabler, grafs market
Gray Adam, wright, horfe wynd
Gray Alexander, taylor, back of theatre
Gray John, baxter, foot of caftle wynd
Gray and Spunkie, milliners, anchor clofe
Gray William, bookfeller, front of Exchange
Gray James, writer, Gosford's clofe
Gray John, writer to the fignet, Miln's fquare
Gray Alexander, writer to fignet, bridge ftreet
Gray James, furveyor, Middleton's entry
Gray David, grocer, foot of the weft bow
Gray Andrew, fhoe-maker, Leith wynd
Gray Robert, procurator, Clelands yards, writing
    chamber, Byers' clofe
Gray George, druggift, op. corn market, S fide
Gray James, teacher of English, &c. bowhead
Gray James, letter-cafe-maker, b of the weigh houfe
Gray James, wright, Nicolfon's ftreet
Gray Robert, writer, Don's clofe, luckenbooths
Gray George, fhoe-maker, potter-row
Gray George, glover, Campbell's clofe, cowgate
Gray James, watch maker, lawn market head
Gray Lord John, Adams' fquare
Gray George, toy merchant, head of Craig's clofe

Gray James, writer, old affembly clofe
Gray Mifs, merchant, luckenbooths
Gray William, ftabler, grafs market
Green William, weaver, oppofite canongate church
Greenfield Alexander, wright, head of Hume's clofe
Greenfield Andrew, minifter, Charles' ftreet
Greenfield William, writer, potter-row
Greenlees Robert, writer, Forrefter's wynd
Greenlees Robert, officer of excife, head of pleafance
Gregory Doctor, St John's ftreet
Greig William, writer, Weir's land, Toderick's wy.
Greig James, writer, Cant's clofe
Greig William, brewer, Campbell's clofe, canongate
Greig John, flefher, canal ftreet
Greig David, grocer, oppofite the college wynd
Greig Alexander, flefher, bull's clofe
Greig David, baker, Shakefpeare fquare
Greig Thomas, baker, abbey
Grieve John, merchant, exchange
Grieve Alexander, book binder, Allan's clofe
Grieve Alexander, wright, caftle-barns
Grieve John, grocer, oppofite meal-market ftairs
Grieve Robert, glazier, weft bow
Grieve Mrs, Nicolfon's ftreet
Grindlay William, mafon, caftle barns
Grindlay John, tanner, portfburgh
Grindly George, leather merchant, f. of weft bow
Guild Mrs, Jolly's clofe caftle-hill
Gull Mifs, Young's ftreet
Gun Donald, writer, St John's ftreet
Gun David, coach hirer, water gate
Gun George, grocer, head of Dickfon's clofe
Guftart Mrs, Morifon's clofe
Guthrie Mrs, room-fetter, old affembly clofe
Guthrie James, fec. to the truftees, exchange
Guthrie Harry, extractor, Alifon's fquare
Guthrie Charles, writer, Libberton's wynd
Guthrie Mrs, old cuftom houfe ftairs
Gwyn Katharine, milliner luckenbooths,

H

Hackfton   Efq; head of pleafance,
Hadow James, general fupervifor of excife, Pirrie's cl.

Haig Mrs, baxter, head of Bull's clofe
Haig Thomas, brewer back of the canongate
Haig James, merchant, Riddle's land
Haig Mrs, merchant, head of luckenbooths
Halden John, writer, Dickfon's clofe
Halden James, vintner, head of advocates clofe
Halden Mifs, fchool-miftrefs, Fowlis' clofe
Halyburton Andrew, writer to the fig Gosford's clofe
Haliday Mrs, Carrubber's clofe
Hall Mifs, of Denglafs, George's fquare
Hall William, merchant, Warrinton's clofe
Hall Thomas, watch-maker, canongate head
Hall John, weaver, Jack's clofe
Hall Mrs, Blyth's clofe, caftle-hill
Hall James, minifter, Gilford's park
Hall John, wig-maker, cowgate-head
Halket Craigie Mrs, oppofite Milton's lodging
Halket Sir John, Willon's court, canongate
Hamilton Robert, of Wilhaw, Efq. St Andrew's ftreet
Hamilton John, Efq. of Readhall, fountain bridge
Hamilton James, merchant, weft bow
Hamilton Major, of Fairholm, fociety
Hamilton Mrs, writers court
Hamilton John, of Bargenny, St Andrew's ftreet
Hamilton-Nifbet Mrs, of Pencaitland, bifhops land
Hamilton Alexander, grocer, head of Leithrwynd
Hamilton the honourable Mrs, St John's ftreet
Hamilton Mrs, of Bangour, water gate
Hamilton John, of Bellifield, Alifon's fquare
Hamilton Mrs, midwife, old affembly clofe
Hamilton Robert, profeffor; near the royal infirmary
Hamilton Robert, brewer, water of Leith
Hamilton Mrs Andrew, ditto
Hamilton Mrs, Adams' fquare
Hamilton Dalrymple and Co. merchants, luckenbooths
Hamilton Mrs, milliner, Miln's fquare
Hamilton James, teacher of mufic, Befs wynd
Hamilton Walter, merchant, cowgate head
Hamilton Captain, Miln's fquare
Hamilton James, Efq. George's fquare
Hamilton James, phyfician, college

Hamilton Mr Andrew, calton hill
Hamilton John, procurator, foot of weſt bow
Hamilton Gavin, water of Leith
Hamilton Mrs, Crichton's ſtreet
Hamilton Alexander, ſurgeon, back ſtairs
Hamilton Mrs, Murdoch's cloſe
Hamilton Mrs, covenant cloſe
Hamilton James, grocer, oppoſite foot of Niddrey's w
Hamilton Mrs, of Fairholm, ſociety
Hamilton Peter, baker, pleaſance
Hamilton Mrs, of ſpittle-haugh, briſto-ſtreet
Hamilton Mrs, teviot row
Hamilton Provoſt Andrew, briſto ſtreet
Hamilton Mrs, Cheſſels' court
Hamilton and Son, upholſterers, tolbooth wynd can,
Hamilton William, wright, pleaſance
Handcock Robert, lace weaver, Dickſon's cloſe
Handcock Mrs, Dickſon's cloſe
Hardie Archibald, ſtabler, graſs market
Hardie James, trunk maker, weſt bow
Hardie George, baxter, bridge ſtreet
Hardie George, baxter, foot of Haſtie's cloſe
Hardie James, writer to ſignet, Semple's cloſe caſtle h
Hardie Andrew, baxter, badgeon hole
Hardie Ralph, baxter, foot of back ſtairs
Hardie George, baxter, near head of Libberton's wynd
Hardie James, brewer, ſouth back of canongate
Hardie John, brewer, pleaſance
Harper William, miniſter, Dickſon's cloſe
Hart Alex cl. of Juſticiary, old cuſtom houſe ſtairs
Hart Orlando, ſhoe-maker, oppoſite the guard
Hart Thomas, ſurgeon, briſto ſtreet
Harvie Thomas, ſtone ware merchant, weſt bow
Haſtie William, ſurgeon, Jackſon's cloſe
Haſtie John, ſmith, Shakeſpeare ſquare
Hay Charles, advocate, Nicolſon's ſtreet
Hay William, jun. writer to the ſignet, Leith wynd
Hay John, accomptant, blackfriars wynd
Hay and Co, grocers, graſs market
Hay Robert, wright and undertaker, advocates cloſe
Hay Alexander, wright, back of exchange
Hay John, captain, St Andrew's ſtreet

Hay James, writer, new ſtreet canongate

Hay James, writer to the ſignet, Libberton's wynd

Hay James, blackfriars wynd

Hay M'Dougal Lady George's ſquare

Hay Peter, wright, chapel ſtreet

Hay James, phyſician, new-ſtreet canongate

Hay George, Eſq; Blackfriars wynd

Hay Thomas, ſurgeon, Strichen's cloſe

Hay Mrs, of Cockla, Nicolſon's ſtreet

Hay John, tackſman of the weigh-houſe, two p. cuſtom

Hay James, Eſq; newington

Hay James writer to the ſignet, Gosford's cloſe

Hay   , ham, cheeſe monger, chandler, and auctio-
     neer, old fiſh market cloſe

Hay Mrs, of Montblery, Niddrey's wynd

Hay John, of Belton, baillie Fyſe's cloſe

Hayſton Lady, potter-row

Hector William, mantua maker, Byres' cloſe lucken.

Handyſide Hugh, baker, luckenbooths

Handyſide Mrs, grocer, cowgate head

Hawthorn Lady, plainſton cloſe, canongate

Hawthorn John, Eſq, Forreſter's wynd

Hawthorn Vance, writer, George's ſquare

Hempſeed Mrs, midwife, foot of weſt bow

Henderſon Bernard, merchant, lawn-market

Henderſon William, brewer, long cloſe pleaſance

Henderſon Peter, grocer, head of the pleaſance

Henderſon Henry fleſher, new fleſh market chapel ſtr.

Henderſon Thomas, iron-monger, weſt bow

Henderſon Sir Robert, St John's ſtreet

Henderſon David, architect, prince's ſtreet

Henderſon Mrs, founder, Stonelaw's cloſe

Henderſon George, merchant, op. foot of old fiſh ma.

Henderſon Mrs, lets rooms, foot of Stonelaw's cloſe

Henderſon Robert ſhoe-maker, foot of the pleaſance

Henderſon John, grocer, foot of Robertſon's cloſe

Henderſon John, grocer, croſs cauſey

Henderſon Mrs, high ſchool yards

Henderſon Mat Eſq, at Mr Vair's barber, at the croſs

Henry Peter, Queen's garden, abbey

Henry Robert, miniſter, Chrichton ſtreet

Henry David, ſhoe-maker, above canongate church

Henry Alexander, grocer, head of Niddery's wynd
Henry Joseph, taylor, Niddrey's wynd
Henry John, excise officer cowgate
Henry John, writer, at Mr Watt's, Forresters wynd
Hepburn Peter, grocer, pleasance
Hepburn George, writer, castle hill
Hepburn Alexander, merchant, Alison's square
Hephurn Thomas, principal session clerk, castle-hill
Hepburn Mrs, Forrester's wynd
Hepburn John, accomptant, Miln's court
Hepburn Mils milliner, front of writers court
Hepburn Mifs, grocer, opposite the tron church
Hepburn John, surgeon, flesh market close, canongate
Hepburn Mrs, Falconer's land canongate
Hepburn Mils, Campbell's land, canongate
Hepburn James, of Humbie Esq; Shakespear's square
Hepburn Mifs, mantua maker, back of the fountain w
Herron Doctor, abbey
Herron Robert shoe-maker, canongate-head
Herriot Thomas, wright, Allan's close
Herriot Archibald, stabler, canongate-head
Herriot John, candle maker, back of the gnard
Herriot James, brewer, goose dub
Herriot George, gun smith, nether bow
Herriot John, writer, Nicolson's street
Hewit James, goldsmith, head of Forrester's wynd
Hill William, wright, Shakespear's square
Hill Thomas, merchant, luckenbooths
Hill Thomas, Shakespeare's square
Hill Mils, milliner, opposite linen hall
Hill David, horse hirer, pleasance
Hill Lawrence, writer, calton hill
Hill Mrs, thread-maker, Forrester's wynd
Hill James, vintner, Kennedy's close
Higgie Thomas, brewer, N. back of canongate
Hodges William, porter-dealer, back of the cross well
Hodge Anthony, baker, foot of Niddery's wynd
Hogg James, wine-merchant, bunkers hill
Hogg Walter, assist. manag linen comp abbey hill
Hogg Mrs, of Harcarse, head of Toderick's wynd
Hogg Thomas, merchant, Riddle's close

Hogg Walter, merchant, back of the meadow
Hogg George, wright, crofs caufey
Hogg Thomas, Efq; George's fquare
Hogg Mrs, Alifon's fquare
Hogg John, fmith, foot of the pleafance
Hogg George, clerk, James' court
Hogg Mrs, grocer, head of plainftone clofe, canongate
Hogg Alexander, merchant, grafs market
Home George, brewer, potter-row
Home Edward, brewer, pleafance
Home George, writer to the fignet, Air bank clofe
Home Francis, profeffor of *materia medica*, Foulis' clofe
Home John, of Ninewells, Efq, St Andrew's fquare
Home George, baxter, at the tron church
Home Lady Jean, Duncan's land, canongate
Home Mrs, George's fquare
Home George,
Home James, writer, Forrefter's wynd
Home Mrs, Forrefter's wynd
Home Henry, writer to the fignet, Jack's land can
Home Mrs, Libberton's wynd
Hope James, wright, Nicolfon's ftreet
Hope Archibald, of Craigie-hall, brifto ftreet
Hope Mifs, mantua-maker, trunk clofe
Hope and Milne, merchants prefident ftairs
Hope John, phyfician, head of high fchool wynd
Hope Archibald, fecretary of the royal bank, newtown
Hope Mrs, and Co. grocers head of Brodie's clofe
Hope Sir Archibald, George's fquare
Hope Mrs, canongate-head
Hope Mrs, of Rankeiller, Jack's land canongate
Horn John, wright, calton hill
Horn James, wright, calton hill
Horfburgh Mrs, milliner, Seller's clofe
Horfburgh Edwin, captain, Jack's clofe
Horfburgh David, phyfician, back of the meadow
Horfburgh Mrs, of Horfburgh, Crichton's entry
Horfburgh Mrs, Jack's land, canongate
Horfman Robert, fupervifor, canongate foot
Horfeman Edward, fupervifor oppofite linen hall
Honeyman   , advocate, cowgate head

G

Hotchkis, James, brewer, grafs market
Houston John, writer, caftle wynd
Houston Nicol, fhoe-maker, foot of Leith wynd
Houston Archibald, carver cowgate-head
Houston Charles, wright, Fisher's clofe, lawn market
Houlton General, Gosford's clofe
Howiefon William, writer, fen. caftle wynd
Howat John, fhoe-maker, potter-row
Howat William, wright, potter-row
Howden John, Blackfriar's wynd
Howden John, grocer, brifto ftreet
Howden John, fadler, grafs market, fouth fide
Howden James, watch-maker, parliament fquare
Houfton Alexander, banker, exchange
Humble John, plumber, prince's ftreet
Hume Lady, canongate foot
Hume William, upholfterer, bridge ftreet
Hume James, lace and fringe maker, Niddery's wynd
Hume John, coach wright, St Andrew's ftreet
Hume John, clerk to the truftees, Richmond ftreet
Hume Mrs, lady Stair's clofe
Hume James, grafier, gibbet toll
Huntington Lady, Strichen's clofe
Hunter William, merchant, head of Carrubers clofe
Hunter James Blair, banker, George's ftreet
Hunter Alexander, merchant, covenant clofe
Hunter Thomas, fhoe-maker, potter-row
Hunter Mrs, late of Thurfton, Miln's court
Hunter Mrs, baxter's clofe
Hunter John, writer to the fignet, queen ftreet
Hunter Robert, of Thurfton, Efq, queen ftreet
Hunter James, hard ware-merchant parliament fquare
Hunter William, furveyor, Monteith's clofe
Hunter Thomas, taylor, canongate-head
Hunter William, flater, Leith wynd
Hunter John, brewer, north back of the canongate
Hunter Charles, bookfeller, Morocco's clofe
Hunter Robert profeffor, college
Hunter Charles, wright,
Hunter William, pewterer, weft-bow foot
Hunter William, grocer, cowgate head
Hunter James, hair-merchant, Thomfon's l. cowgate

Hunter James, physician, old bank close
Hunter Richard, turner, Turk's close
Hunter M s, room setter, post house stairs
Hunter Adam, grocer, lawn market
Hunter Thomas, taylor, Leith wynd
Hunter Mrs, Paterson's court
Hunter William, Hyndford's close
Hunter Mrs, Jack's land canongate
Hutchison Mrs, bow-head
Hutchison Thomas, merchant, foot of Kinloch's close
Hutchison Mrs, Herriot's bridge
Hutchison Mrs, Kinloch's close
Hutchison Mrs, Forrester's wynd
Hutchison Alex. merchant, first stair below bridge-street
Hutchison and son, merchants luckenbooths
Hutchison Thomas, baxter, opposite the guard
Hutchison John, Scot's close, cowgate
Hutchison Robert, officer of excise, plea'ance
Hutchison John Stay maker, Ramsay's land, canongate
Hutchison William, druggist, cowgate head
Hutton Miss, milliner, front of exchange
Hutton Mrs, china merchant, exchange
Hutton John, stationer, parliament square
Hutton David, taylor, portsburgh
Hutton James, clock and watch maker, portsburgh
Hutton James physician, St John's hill
Hutton Miss, musician, Kennedy's close
Husband, Elder, and Co. confectioners, op. tron church
Husband James, stabler, cowgate head
Hyndford Earl of, advocate, St John's street

I

Imbrie Alexander, staymaker, potter row
Imbrie Robert, hair dresser, St Mary's wynd
Inch James, smith, high-school wynd
Inglis Sir John, opposite Magdalen chapel
Inglis Mrs, of orchard-field, Chalmers close
Inglis Miss, Charles' street
Inglis Miss, Gordon's land, grass market
Inglis George, Esq, of Read hall, back-row
Inglis and Dewar, surgeons, luckenbooths
Inglis Charles, dep cl. to bills, old custom house stairs
Inglis Lawrence, writer, Heriot's bridge

Inglis and Horner, merchants, old cuſtom houſe ſtairs
Inglis Claud, merchant, luckenbooths
Inglis James, grocer, weſt port
Inglis Mrs foot of Kinloch's cloſe
Inglis Gilbert, writer & ſchool-maſt. f. of Libberton'sw,
Inglis William, wright, canongate-head
Inglis Archibald, pewterer, Kennedy's cloſe
Inglis John, ſchool maſter, upper common cloſe can.
Inglis Mrs, Hanover ſtreet
Inglis Hugh, wig-maker, portſburgh
Innes George, ſtamp office,
Innes Mrs, of Urull, St Andrew's ſquare
Innes George, of Stow, Miln's court
Innes Alexander, writer to the ſignet, St David's ſtr.
Innes Edward, baker, ten. head of fleſh market cloſe
Innes Edward, jun. baker, head of Cant's cloſe
Innes Francis, gun-ſmith, cowgate-head
Innes James, wig maker, Caitchen's land, cowgate
Innes Charles, merchant, at the croſs
Innes Charles, writer, firſt ſtair below tron church
Innes Mrs, Blackfriar's wynd
Innes Mrs, Cant's cloſe
Innes John, writer to the ſignet, foot of Kinloch's cl.
Innes Mrs, briſto-ſtreet
Innes George, wright, pleaſance
Innes Thomas, writer to the ſignet, advocates cloſe
Inverarity James, grocer, cowgate-head
Inverarity David, wright, canal ſtreet
Ireland James, baker, pleaſance
Ireland George, James' court
Irvine George, Eſq, Briſto-ſtreet
Irvine James, of Kincouſſie, Nicolſon's ſtreet
Irvine John, prin. clerk to the chancery, Miln's court
Irvine William, writer, Gosford's cloſe
Irvine Daniel, turner, fiſh market cloſe
Irvine Mrs, Somervill's land canongate
Irvine Robert, writer, calton hill
Iver David, grocer, croſs-cauſey
Izet James, hatter, Morrocco's land, canongate

J

Jack William, hoſier, oppoſite foot of Libberton's wy.
Jack Andrew, vintner, writer's court

Jack Thomas, stabler, cowgate head

Jackson Will. sec. to the post office, Carruber's close

Jackson and Gourlay, haberdashers, head of old fish m

Jackson Mrs, covenant close

Jackson Miss, Nicolson's street

Jackson Mrs, Forrester's wynd

Jamieson Robert, writer to the signet, Wardrop's court

Jamieson John, excise, Buchanan's court

Jamieson Mrs, boarding house, Buchanan's court

Jamieson William, mason, Lady Stairs' close

Jamieson George, tabbacconist, grafs-market S. side

Jamieson Robert, bookseller, parliament square

Jarden John, from Dumfries, Niddery's wynd

Jarvie Doctor, Henderson's stairs

Jeffrey Francis and James, wig makers, lawn-market

Jeffrey William, grocer, back of the bow head well

Jeffrey George, writer, Fishers land

Jenkens   , school master, Forresters wynd

Johnstone William, wright, bull close

Johnstone James, engraver, Reoch's land

Johnstone Wynn, of Hilton, Chrichton's entry

Johnstone Mrs, St Andrew's street

Johnstone Charles, school master, excise office, canon.

Johnstone Miss, Sophia, Chrichton street

Johnstone Major James, Nicolson's street

Johnstone John, writer, James' court

Johnstone Robert, currier, S. back of canongate

Johnstone John, wine-merchant, first baxter's close

Johnstone William, school master, Wardrop's court

Johnstone John, founder, calton

Johnston Robert, banker, front of exchange

Johnstone John, writer, Morison's close

Johnstone William, mason, college wynd

Johnstone James, stay maker, St Mary's wynd

Johnstone Charles, stay-maker, Reoch's land cowgate

Johnstone Alexander, shoe maker, Robertson's close

Johnstone William, shoe-maker, bristo-street

Johnstone William, hair-dresser, h. of bailie Fyfe's cl.

Johnstone Mrs, grocer, bowhead

Johnstone Mrs, west bow

Johnstone Alexander, of Straiton, St David's street

Johnstone Captain Mrs, Nicolson's street

Johnstone Mrs, Somervill's land canongate
Johnstone Mrs, midwife, James' court
Johnstone Hugh, mason, cowgate
Johnstone Miss, boarding mistress, Fowlis' close
Johnstone Robert, hair dresser, head of Chalmers' close
Johnstone Walter, stabler, Paterson's land, grass m.
Johnstone Andrew, stabler, west-bow foot
Johnstone Andrew, grocer, bristo street
Johnstone Mrs, midwife, anchor close
Jop James, taylor, tolbooth wynd canongate
Jolly James, writer, bailie Fyfe's close
Jolly Andrew taylor, canongate, head
Jollie George, taylor, canongate-head, south side
Jollie Mrs, taylor, bailie Fyfe's close
Justice Mrs, canongate-head
Justice Mrs, room-letter, Gavinloch's land

K

Kay Alexander, writer, Robertson's close, cowgate
Kay John, brewer, Robertson's close, cowgate
Kay John, hair-dresser, above the guard, north side
Kay James, writer, Robertson's close cowgate
Kay Robert, writer, Robertson's close
Kay George, Esq; bristo
Kay Mrs, Alison's square
Keddie Alexander, candle-maker, h. Libberton's wy.
Keeling and Co's stone-ware room, bridge street
Keir Adam, baxter, opposite the Exchange
Keirs Mrs, Alison's close
Keith Misses, Shakespeare square
Keith Alexander, depute clerk of Session, college wy
Keith William, accomptant, head of Blackfriars wynd
Keith Mrs, Shakespeare's square
Keggie John, stocking maker, corn market
Kellie John, wright, bristo-street
Kellie Mrs, white iron smith, west bow
Kelly Mils, perfumer, opposite bow head well
Keltie John, hair-dresser, Morison's close
Kempt Gavin, merchant, Reid's close, canongate
Kempt James, merchant, head of Reid's close
Kempt John, minister, Wilson's court canongate
Kempt Alexander, writer, castle hill
Kemptie Francis, canongate sugar house

Kennedy Mrs, of Kilhainine, fountain clofe
Kennedy Mrs, Campbell's land, canongate
Kennedy Mifs, Shakefpeare fquare
Kennedy Robert, merchant, blackfriars wynd
Kennedy Walter and Robert, coopers, potter-row
Kennedy Thomas, glover, creams
Kennedy Robert, taylor, chapel ftreet
Kennedy Francis, grocer, foot of Forrefter's wynd
Kennedy Miffes, milliners, horfe wynd
Kennedy Mrs, foot of Robertfon's clofe
Kennedy Mrs, Crichton's ftreet
Kerr Robert, captain, new town
Kerr William, of Chatto, high fchool yards
Kerr William, of Abbotrule, writer to fig. Brown's fq.
Kerr Mrs, weft kirk brae-head
Kerr James, keeper of the records, lauriefton
Kerr Thomas, hair dreffer, blackfriars wynd
Kerr William, clerk in the poft office, bowhead
Kerr George, tin plate worker, nether bow
Kerr Mrs, Merlin's wynd
Kerr Walter, land meafurer, Dickfon's clofe
Kerr Mrs, mantua-maker, Toderick's wynd
Kerr Mrs, grocer, oppofite canongate church
Kerr Mrs, oppofite linen hall
Kerr James, of Black-Shields, fhoe makers clofe, can.
Kerr John, of Keavers, Cant's clofe
Kettle James, writer, head of Libberton's wynd
Key William, architect, Shakefpeare's fquare
Key John, Efq, Alifon's fquare
Key George, grocer, Reoch's land, cowgate
Kid John, wine-merchant, cowgate-head
Kid Alex. writer, at J. Braidwood's, new ftreet
Kigie James, grocer, St Mary's wynd
Kilgour Alexander, taylor, flefh market clofe
Kilpatrick John, merchant, head of old bank clofe
King John, writer, Hanover ftreet
Kincaid Alexander, writer, potter-row
Kinloch David, of Gilmerton, Efq, exchange
Kinloch John, white iron fmith, weft bow
Kinloch Robert, of Kinmoth, Efq; Blackfriars wynd
Kinloch Hugh, grocer, head of Air bank clofe
Kinloch Robert, glover, creams

Kinnaird William, druggift, foot of horfe wynd
Kinnear and Son, infurance brokers, front of exchange
Kinnear Robert, Geddes' clofe
Kinnear Andrew, pewterer, lawn market, N. fide
Kinnear George, hofier, f. of Robertfon's clofe cowg,
Kinnear Mrs, Skinners clofe
Kinniburgh William, candle-maker, caftle-hill
Kinniburgh Robert, glazier, Borthwick's clofe foot
Kinrofs Charles, hair-dreffer, brifto ftreet
Kirk Thomas, dyer, Paul's work
Kirkaldie David, ftay-maker, Toderick's wynd
Kirkner George, teacher of mufic, Bell's wynd
Kirkland James, accomptant, laurifton
Kirkland Mrs, weft port
Kirkpatrick George, dep. clerk of feffion, Crichton ftr,
Kitchen William, fchool-mafter, potter-row
Knight John, ftabler, grafs market
Knox David, bari-keeper, lawn market
Knox Mrs, uppermoft baxter's clofe
Knox Mrs, weft bow foot
Knox Mifs, mantua-maker, oppofite linen hall

L

Laidlaw James, writer, Barrenger's clofe
Laidlaw Alexander, tin plate worker, weft bow
Laidlay John, tin-plate worker, weft bow
Laidley John, candle maker, St Ninian's row
Laing George, writer, Campbell's clofe cowgate
Laing Alexander, mafon, bunkers hill
Laing Thomas, tool-maker, Shakefpeare fquare
Laing Mrs, vintner, Don's clofe
Laing Robert, faddler, head of Murdoch's clofe
Laing Thomas, vintner, Borthwick's clofe
Laing William, phyfician, Carrubber's clofe
Laing James, writer, council chamber, Warrifton's cl.
Lake Richard, wine-merchant, St Andrew's fquare
Lake Richard, writer, St Andrew's ftreet
Lamb William, upholfterer, head of Gray's clofe
Lamb John, hofier, head of Toderick's wynd
Lamb Mifs, mantua-maker, Niddery's wynd
Lamond Alexander, grocer, head of the pleafance
Landels William, filk dyer, canongate-head
Langlands Robert, phyfician, Shakefpeare fquare

Langlands John, linen-manufacturer, Charles street
Laurie John, school master, Nicolson's street
Laurie William, upholsterer, lawn-market, north side
Lauchlan Joseph, merchant above Dunbar's close
Lauder James, of Carrollside, Esq; old post house close
Lauder & Dryfdale, stay & habit makers, Leith wynd
Lauder Mrs. candle-maker, below Cheffels' court
Lauder James, shoe-maker, Nicolson's street
Lauder John, coperfmith, west-bow
Lauder Mrs, Riddle's close
Lauder Colin, surgeon, bridge street
Laurie Gilbert, senr. commiffi. of excife, cowgate-h,
Laurie and Co. druggifts, head of Niddrey's wynd
Laurie John, lint-dreffer, crofs caufey
Laurie Robert, school master, oppofite meal market
Laurie Robert, clerk in the excife, laurieston
Laurie William, writer, at Mr Marfhal's Miln's fq.
Laurie Andrew, dancing-master, Carrubber's clofe
Laurie William, writer, laurieston
Law John, meffenger, head of Bell's wynd
Law Mrs, Periie's clofe, canongate
Law Alexander, advocate, Adams' court
Law William, writer, Adams' court
Lawder Mrs. Riddle's clofe
Law William, merchant, luckenbooths
Lawfon George, weaver, Leith wynd
Lawfon James, leather merch. lawn market, N. fide
Learmonth John, tanner, St Mary's wynd
Learmonth Mifs, milliner, Carruber's clofe
Learmonth Colville, Leith walk
Leaverock Mrs Peggy, grocer, op. Toderick's wynd
Le Brun John, French teacher, Miln's fquare
Lee Patrick, grocer, head of Burnet's clofe
Le Grand Richard, Efq. Bonneytown
Legget James vintner, new bank clofe
Leighton Alexander, stay-maker, canongate head
Leighton John, merchant, luckenbooths
Leighton Mrs, Charles' street
Leifhman James, bookbinder, Gosford's clofe
Leith Mrs of Overfhall, George's fquare
Leith Peter, taylor, Prince's street

Leitch Mrs, grocer, head of Libberton's wynd
Leith Patrick, wright, pleasance
Lennox William, of Woodhead, Esq; at lin. hall, can.
Lerry William, broker, netherbow
Leslie Mrs, of Aiton, middle of canongate
Leslie-Dugud Mrs, Bunker's-hill
Leslie George, Esq. Hanover street
Leslie Mrs, bristo street
Leslie William, writer to the signet, high-school yards
Leslie James, Reikie's land, Nicolson's street
Leslie John, writer, blackfriar's wynd
Leslie Charles, procurator, blackfriar' wynd
Leslie George, merchant, Shakespeare's square
Leslie John, Captain, Don's close
Leslie Patrick, musician, Dickson's close
Lethem Thomas, smith, grass-market, south side
Leven the Earl of, Nicolson's square
Leven the Countess Dowager of, St Andrew's street
Lewis Miss, Charles street
Liddle   , carver and gilder, candle-maker-row
Lind James, physician, Prince's street
Lind William, musical instrument maker, Skinner's cl.
Lind James, shoe-maker, St Mary's wynd
Lind William, upholsterer, Bunker's-hill
Lindsay Mrs, bristo street
Lindsay David, Abbey
Lindsay Patrick, Esq, St John's street
Lindsay Henry, merchant, east end of luckenbooths
Lindsay David, writer, castle hill
Lindsay Martin, writer, back of the meadows
Lindsay, Anderson, and Co. merchants, luckenbooths
Lindsay Thomas, stabler, foot of Libberton's wynd
Lindsay David, skinner, bow-head
Lindsay George, grocer, at the canongate church
Lindsay Mrs mantua-maker, horse wynd
Lindsay John, wire-worker, castle hill
Lindsay Mrs, room-setter, opposite bridge street
Lindsay Mrs, room-setter, Craig's close
Linton James, grocer, bristo street
Liston Mat. teacher of mathemat hammer. land, co.
Little John, clerk, St Mary's wynd
Little William, writer, Miln's court

Little William.Charles, advocate, Brown's fquare
Livingftone Charles, writer, Nicolfon's ftreet
Livingftone James, writing-mafter, weft-bow
Livingftone Alexander, grocer, crofs caufey
Lizars Daniel, engraver, head of Bell's wynd
Lizars Mifs, mantua-maker bifhop's land clofe
Loch David, of Over-carnbee, St Ann's yards
Loch James, writer to the fignet, Paterfon's court
Loch William, writer, Paterfon's court
Lockhart Thomas, of excife, George's fquare
Lockhart lady, fountain-bridge
Lockhart Mrs, of Birkhill, Nicolfon's ftreet
Lockhart Mrs, of Cleghorn, cowgate head
Lockhart James, writer, op. blackfriar's wynd
Lockhart William, writer, brifto ftreet
Lockhart William, fhoe-maker, cowgate head
Lockhart-Rofs, George's fquare
Logan Robert, book-binder, weft-bow-foot
Logie Mrs, canal ftreet
Lothian Mrs, teacher of Englifh, upperm baxter's cl.
Lothian Mifs, Buccleugh's ftreet
Lothian Edward, goldfmith, St John's hill
Lothian William, minifter, St John's hill
Lothian George, blackfriars wynd
Lothian David, writer, Riddle's clofe, lawn-market
Lothian John, merchant, exchange
Lothian Mrs, midwife, Toderick's wynd
Lovat lady, blackfriars wynd
Low James, filk-ayer, Douglas' clofe, grafs market
Low John, grocer, head of Skinner's clofe
Low Alexr. wig maker, op. head of Halkerfton's w.
Lowrie William, cutler, op. foot of Forrefter's wynd
Lowrie William, tool-maker, potter-row
Lowrie Andrew, writing mafter, Campbell's clofe
Lowrie John, fchool-mafter, Nicolfon's ftreet
Lowrie William, fhoe maker, foot of the pleafance
Lowrifton Mrs, crofs caufey
Lorrimer Mrs, taylor, Nicolfon's ftreet
Loyed Mrs, Skinner's clofe
Luke James, baxter, brifto-ftreet
Lumifdaine James, of Renny hill, new ftreet

Lumsden Mrs, of Innergally, St John's street
Lumsden Miss, Stonelaw's close
Lundie Misses, Forrester's wynd
Lundie Mrs, of Kelly, prince's street
Lundie Henry, minister, Forrester's wynd
Lundie Michael writer, Skinner's close
Lundie Mrs, of Auchtermairney, St John's street
Lyon Major Andrew, chapel street
Lyon Mrs, embroiderer, fountain close
Lyon William, grocer, high-school wynd
Lyon William, stabler, candle-maker-row

M

Mabon William, cutler and armourer, west port
Mack John, writer, foot of South Gray's close
Mack Joseph, grocer, head of the pleasance
Mackie Charles, goldsmith, potter-row port
Main David, taylor, abbey-strand
Mair Gilbert, extractor, bailie Fyfe's close
Mair Thomas, merchant, Merlin's wynd
Mair Mrs, Kincaid's land
Mair Mrs, Sellars' close
Maitland Captain, laurieston
Maitland Mrs, of Petrichie, bailie Fyfe's close
Maitland Mrs, St John's street
Maitland Miss, mantua-maker, Nidry's wynd
Maitland Dr, St Andrew's street
Maitland Alexander, grocer, west-bow
Maitland John, bunker's hill
Maitland Robert, surgeon, St Andrew's street
Malcolm William, wright, Leith walk
Malcolm David, shoe-maker, canongate-head
Malcolm Thomas, shoe maker, hammermen's land, cow.
Malcolm Mrs, midwife, Moffat's close, nether-bow
Malcolm William, stay-maker, flesh market close, can.
Malcolm George, shoe-maker, old playhouse close
Malcolm John, writer, foot of Dickson's close
Maltman James, druggist, foot of Forrester's wynd
Mann Mrs, post house stairs
Manners Alexander, head of Kennedy's close
Mansfield Mrs, Reid's close, canongate
Mansfield, Ramsay, and Co. bankers, luckenbooths
Mansfield Mrs, Carrubber's close

Manson Thomas, writer, baillie Fyfe's close
Manuel Hugh, writer, causey-side
March the ladies of, Miln's square
March James, shoe maker, Paul's work
Marcucia Madam, James' court
Marchbanks Captain, blackfriar's wynd
Marjoribanks Alexander, of that ilk, Foulis's close
Marnoch James, senr hosier, op. the fountain well
Marr William, smith, king's stables, portsburgh
Marshall Andrew, leather cutter, cross causey
Marshall Francis, hard-ware merchant, luckenbooths
Marshall James, writer to the signet, Miln's square
Marshall David, goldsmith, canal street
Marshall Alexander, taylor, Nicolson's street
Marshall John, grocer, Nicolson's street
Marshall John, shoe maker, potter-row
Marshall Mrs, keeps boarders, bristo street
Marshall Mrs, room setter, mint close
Martin William, grocer, head of Chambers' close
Martin James, musician, Foderick's wynd
Martin George, writer, Argyle's square
Martin Robert, vintner, covenant close
Martin Thomas, founder, foot of Leith wynd
Martin John, merchant, bristo street
Martin Gilbert, printer, pleasance
Martin William, shoe maker, flesh market close, can.
Martin Robert, vintner, Roxburgh's close
Martin Samuel, lapper, west-bow
Martin Charles, barber, bow-head well
Martin William, bookseller, west-bow
Mason Alexander, writer, back of the guard
Mason John, merchant, luckenbooths
Mason William, extractor, back of the weigh-house
Mason Gilbert, merchant, St Andrew's square
Mason John, baker, opposite blackfriars wynd
Mason John, baker and grocer, below can. church
Mason John, baker, cowgate-head
Mason James, grocer, head of Skinner's close
Mason Alexander, school master, Carruber's close
Mason Arthur, teacher of languages, old assembly cl.
Mason James, china man, bridge-street
Mason John, writer, Morocco's close, canongate

Mason James, grocer, Cheſſel's land, canongate
Mason Mrs, Libberton's wynd
Mason William, merchant, head of old bank cloſe
Maſterton Allan, writing-maſter, Stonelaws cloſe
Maſterton Dougall, writing-maſter, oppoſite the guard
Mather Robert, grocer, foot of Robertſon's cloſe
Mathie John, wright, college wynd
Matthew Thomas, cl. in the poſt office, Carrub. cl.
Matthie John, baker, oppoſite canongate church
Matthie and Hunter, grocers, above Carrub. cloſe
Matthew John, vintner, fleſh market cloſe
Matthew John, writer, Graſs market
Mathew James, writer at Mr Willon's royal bank cl.
Matthieſon James, writer, op. Queenſberry lodging
Maughan John, clerk in the excheq. kirkbrae-head
Maule David, taylor, college wynd
Maxwell Hugh, writer, prince's ſtreet
Maxwell Archibald, writer, James' court
Maxwell lady, of Pollock, prince's ſtreet
Maxwell Alexander, wine-merchant, George's ſq.
Maxwell David, Eſq. advocate, Don's cloſe
Maxwell Miſs, of Dalſwinton, blackfriars wynd
Maxwell David, advocate, Richmond ſtreet
Maxwell Mrs, of Gairdineſs, Gabriel's road
Maxwell lady Dowager, of Monreith, walk of Leith
Maxwell Mrs, Paterſon's court
Mayelſton and Co. merchants. exchange
Mayelſton Mrs, grocer, St Andrew's ſtreet
M'Adam James, taylor, Skinner's cloſe
M'Anſh Alexander, potter-row
M'Arthur Archibald, advocate, Fiſher's cl. lawn m.
M'Arthur Mrs, room-ſetter, lawn market
M'Arthur Archibald, Eſq; Fiſher's cloſe
M'Alaſter Miſs, blackfriars wynd
M'Call James, wright, head of the pleaſance
M'Call James, grocer, Nicolſon's ſtreet
M'Call   , ſhoe-maker, oppoſite bow-head
M'Call Hugh, writer, Hyndtord's cloſe
M'Call John, grocer, St Agnes ſtreet
M'Callum John, ſteward to the king's cutter, below
   Queenſberry lodging
M'Caſlan Mrs, bookſeller, croſs cauſey,

M'Cara Andrew, grocer, foot of Niddery's wynd
M'Conochie Alexander, advocate, fociety
M'Conochie Allan, advocate. James' court
M'Conochie William, wright, Hanover ftreet
M'Cormack Edward, advocate, oldcuftom-houfe ftairs
M'Credie John, grocer, Crichton ftreet
M'Culloch, filk manufactory, potter-row
M'Dairmed John, fpirit dealer, Kincaid's l. cowgate
M'Donald Archibald, advocate, James' court
M'Donald William, writer to the fignet Adams' court
M'Donald Thomas, writer, oppofite to General's entry
M'Donald Mrs, druggift, head of lady Stairs' clofe
M'Donald James, dancing-mafter, lawn market
M'Donald Andrew, grocer, canongate-head
M'Donald Captain, Hyndford's clofe
M'Donald John, grocer, head of Strichan's clofe
M'Donald Mrs, mantua-maker, weft bow head
M'Donald George, lint dreffer, pleafance
M'Donald Alexander, fmith caftle-hill
M'Donald, Donald, grocer, head of St Mary's wynd
M'Donald John, lint-dreffer, horfe wynd
M'Donald Donald, barber, head of the pleafance
M'Donald Allan, writer to the fignet, Miln's fquare
M'Donald Lord, George's ftreet, new town
M'Donald Daniel, back of the guard
M'Donald Archibald, glafier, foot of Libberton's wy.
M'Donald Angus, cloth merchant, lawn market
M'Donald Mrs, Shakefpeare fquare
M'Donald Major, Shakefpeare fquare
M'Donald Daniel, grocer, cowgate-head
M'Donald Alex. writer to fignet, Libberton's wynd
M'Donald James, mufician, caftle-hill.
M'Dougall Alex. dep. remembrancer, Efq; fountain cl.
M'Dougall Alexander, writer, college wynd
M'Dougall Patrick, writer, ldy Stairs' clofe
M'Dougall James, taylor, crofs caufey
M'Dougall James, taylor, op. chapel of eafe
M'Dowall James, Efq, canon mills
M'Dowall Mrs, Kinloch's clofe
M'Dowall Archibald, clothier, bridge-ftreet
M'Dowall William, ftocking-maker, weft bow

M'Ewan Mrs, south Gray's close
M'Ewan William, writer, old excise office cowgate
M'Ewan William, grocer, St Andrew's street
M'Ewan William, spirit dealer, foot of college wy.
M'Fait Ebenezer, mathematician, below f of horse wy
M'Farlane William, of that ilk, Bryden's close can.
M'Farlane Duncan, foot of the pleasance
M'Farlane Andrew, stabler, cowgate head
M'Farlanes Miss, mantua-makers, Carrubber's close
M'Farlane William, writer, Gavinloch's land lucken.
M'Farlane James, taylor, mint close
M'Farlane Walter, grocer, foot of Stonelaw's close
M'Farlane John, minister, Lochend's close
M'Farlane Mrs, of Fairnyside, George's square
M'Farlane George, stabler, grass market
M'Farlane Daniel, brewer, portsburgh
M'Farlane John, distiller, Jack's close canongate
M'Farquhar Colin, printer, Hunters park
M'Farquhar George, coach painter, Leith wynd
M'Farquhar James, wig-maker, New town
M'Gachen Robert, hosier, east wing of the exchange
M'George Thomas, baker, grass market
M'Ghie Mrs, Hanover square
M'Gibbon and Logan, merchants, luckenbooths
M'Glashan Alexander, musician, Skinners close
M'Gowan John, writer, east end of luckenbooths
M'Gowan Mrs, grocer, foot of Dickson's close
M'Grew Mrs, baker, potter-row
M'Grigor George, grocer, opposite St John's street
M'Grigor Alexander, vintner, Brown's close
M'Grigor Alexander, spirit dealer, foot of fish market
M'Grougar Thomas, grocer, Riddle's land lawn m.
M'Harg Mrs, new town
M'Hattie William, grocer, below canongate church
M'Hattie Alexander, grocer, head of canongate
M'Intosh John, clerk to royal bank, Crichton street
M'Intosh Peter, messenger, back of Beils wynd
M'Intosh Andrew, starch manufactorer, canongate
M'Intosh Robert, musician, Barrenger's close
M'Intosh John, barber, Peebles wynd
M'Intosh John, fishing rod maker, canongate-head

M‘Intosh Charles, writer, thistle court
M‘Intosh Alexander, grocer, head of canongate
M‘Intyre John, teacher of languages, op. meal market
M‘Intyre Daniel, spirit dealer, Stonelaws close
M‘Kain David, merchant, Nicolfon's street
M‘Kay Mrs, of Bighoufe, canongate
M‘Kay Donald, taylor, Shakefpeare fquare
M‘Kay the honourable Mifs, teviot row
M‘Kay Henry, fupervifor, brifto street
M‘Kay George, vintner, calton
M‘Kay General, George's fquare
M‘Kay Henry, fupervifor, brifto street
M‘Kell James, fifh hook maker, Leith wynd
M‘Kell Hugh, writer, Hyndford's clofe
M‘Kell Robert, John's clofe canongate
M‘Kell Charles, from Jamaica, Leith wynd
M‘Keal William, writer, at Mrs Gibb's meal market
M‘Kenzie Kenneth, of Seaforth, abbey
M‘Kenzie Mrs, of Applecrofs, wind mill street
M‘Kenzie Mis, merchant, luckenbooths
M‘Kenzie Kenneth, writer to the fignet luckenbooths
M‘Kenzie Henry, attorney of exchequer, Brown's fq;
M‘Kenzie John, advocate, St Andrew's street
M‘Kenzie Jofeph, phyfician, cowgate-head
M‘Kenzie Mrs, oyster-cellar, front of Adams' fquare
M‘Kenzie Mrs, canongate-foot
M‘Kenzie Mrs, grocer, canongate
M‘Kenzie Mrs William, new street
M‘Kenzie William, taylor, back of the guard
M‘Kenzie Charles, writer, Byers' clofe
M‘Kenzie Kenneth, druggift, head of Cant's clofe
M‘Kenzie Mifs, milliner, Blackfriars wynd
M‘Kenzie Duncan, fhoe-maker, Reoch's land, cowg.
M‘Kenzie John, taylor, Leith wynd
M‘Kenzie Mrs, room-letter, old affembly clofe
M‘Kenzie John, of the cuftom-houfe, chapel street
M‘Kenzie James, jeweler, parliament fquare
M‘Kenzie Andrew, writer, horfe wynd
M‘Kenzie Alexander, writer, Carrubber's clofe
M‘Kenzie Roderick, baker, head of St John's street
M‘Kindlay Mrs, midwife, Kinloch's clofe

M'Kinlay George, room-setter, college wynd
M'Kinnon Daniel, peruke maker, luckenbooths
M'Kinnon Neal, barber, Strichen's clofe
M'Laggan Robert, writer, lawn market
M'Laggan Mrs, midwife, fountain clofe
M'Laren Dougal, writer, parliament fquare
M'Laren Daniel, turner, fountain well
M'Laren James, mufician, Toderick's wynd
M'Laren Hector, fhoe-maker, Dickfon's clofe
M'Lauchlan Duncan, fhoe-maker, head of pleafance
M'Laurin John, advocate, George's fquare
M'Leay Thomas, extractor, Dalrymple's office
M'Leay William, grocer, potter-row
M'Lean Hugh, of Kingerloch, chaple ftreet
M'Lean Captain Murdoch, canongate
M'Lean Carnegy, ftatuary & print feller, Nidderys w.
M'Lean Mrs, Libberton's wynd
M'Lean William, merchant, luckenbooths
M'Lean Donald, feed merchant, h. of anchor clofe
M'Lean Duncan, grocer, Thomfon's land cowgate.
M'Lean William, hair dreffer, Campbell's clofe cow.
M'Lean George, fly-hook dreffer, nether bow
M'Lean Mrs, room-letter, briffo-ftreet
M'Lean Mrs, Millers land canongate
M'Lean Lauchlan, merc. head of old play houfe clofe
M'Lean James, taylor, St Mary's wynd
M'Lean John, merchant, Warrifton's clofe
M'Lean Mrs, writers court
M'Lean George, clock and watch maker, briffo ?
M'Lean Mifs, mantua maker, foot of Leith wynd
M'Lean William, dancing-mafter, Niddery's wynd
M'Lean Robert, clerk in the excife office drumfheugh
M'Leifh James, bookfeller, candle-maker-row
M'Leifh Adam, merchant, foot of Niddery's wynd
M'Leifh Daniel, ftone ware merchant, Bifhop's land
M'Leifh Adam, merchant, oppofite Niddery's wynd
M'Lellan Mrs, of Barfcob, Weir's clofe canongate
M'Lellan James, faddler, foot of crofs cauley
M'Leod-Bannantyne William, advocate, Craig's clofe
M'Leod William, of Offe, twopenny cuftom
M'Leod Roderick, writer to the fignet, Craig's clofe

M'Leod Roderick, jun. Niddery's wynd
M'Leod Mrs, of M'Leod, St Andrew's ftreet
M'Leod Daniel, grocer, head of Libberton's wynd
M'Leod Mrs, of Cadboll, caftle hill
M'Leur John, writing-mafter, Paterfon's court
M'Martin Malcolm, fpirit dealer, Miln's fquare
M'Michan William, fchool mafter, calton
M'Millan Duncan, of morningfide, James' court
M'Millan Mrs, James' court
M'Millan Robert, paper ftainer, Miln's fquare
M'Millan Wil writer in excheq. Falconer's land can.
M'Nab and M'Donald, haberdafhers, op. new bridge
M'Nab William, glazier, head of the plainftone clofe
M'Nab John, writer, trunk clofe
M'Nab Peter, fifh monger, fifh market clofe
M'Nab Charles, grocer, head of Barranger's clofe
M'Naught James, confectioner, foot of horfe wynd
M'Naughton Malc. hard ware mer. h. of Allan's cl.
M'Naughton James, ftabler, cowgate head
M'Night James, minifter, Nicolfon's ftreet
M'Night Samuel, Chalmers' clofe
M'Phell Miles, vintner, Fowlis' clofe
M'Pherfon Norman, watch-maker, h. of covenant cl.
M'Pherfon John, mufician, Bell's wynd
M'Pherfon William, ftocking maker, candle-maker-r
M'Pherfon, mafon, canal ftreet
M'Pherfon William, writer, canal ftreet
M'Pherfon David, writer, caftle hill
M'Pherfon Mrs, room-fetter, Gosford's clofe
M'Pherfon John, vintner, Niddery's wynd
M'Pherfon and Co. woollen-drapers, princes ftreet
M'Phie Mrs, weft bow head
M'Phie Donald, hair dreffer, grafs market
M'Queen James, writer, flefh market clofe
M'Queen Mrs, white-iron fmith, nether bow
M'Queen John and Co. feeds men, laurieston
M'Queen George, Cefs-office, new town
M'Queen William, baker, Nicolfon's ftreet
M'Quiven Mrs, ftay-maker, canongate-head
M'Redie John, grocer, Crichton ftreet
M'Target Thomas, fpirit-dealer, abbey
M'Tearn James, mufician, blackfriars wynd

M'Vicar Neil, writer, trunk clofe
M'Vicar Neil and Co. hnes manufacturers, potter row
M'Vicar Patrick, writer, Hamilton's entry, brifto ft.
Maitland Robert, furgeon, St Andrew's ftreet
Meals Mrs, room-letter, potter-row
Meafon Gilbert, Efq, St Andrew's fquare
Meekifon Mifs, milliner, pleafance
Meekifor David, hatter, pleafance
Megget J. currier and leather merch. foot of pleaf,
Meikle Robert, writer, Leith wynd
Meikle Andrew, taylor, oppofite Cheffels' court
Meikle John, ftabler, bull's clofe
Mein Andrew, grocer, Fifher's land, lawn market
Mein Beaument, writer, St Leonards
Merry James Owen, doctor of phyf old cuft. h ftairs
Meldrum Mrs, op. linen hall, canongate
Mellis James, writer, trunk clofe
Mellis George, flefher, flefh market clofe
Mellis Andrew, flefher, flefh market clofe
Mellis Peter, flefher, flefh market clofe
Mellis William, flefher, flefh market clofe
Mellis Thomas, flefher, flefh market clofe
Mellis John, flefher, prince's ftreet
Melvill Thomas, fhoe maker, op. Cheffel's court
Melvill Mrs, weft bow
Mennons John, printer, Brodie's clofe, lawn market
Menzies Mrs, of Culterallers, Crichton ftreet
Menzies Mrs, blackfriars wynd
Menzies Mrs, Nicolfon's ftreet
Menzies William, folicitors clerk of cuft. calton hill
Menzies Alexr. writer to the fignet, Carruber's clofe
Menzies Douglas, fhoe maker, general's ent. potter r,
Menzies Alexander, ftabler, candle-maker-row
Menzies Mrs, of Cuidares, New town
Menzies Robert, ftamp-office
Menzies Robert, writer, Robertfon's clofe
Menzies Mrs, of Belmaduffie, Aitken's land, canong.
Mercer William, merchant, op. the tron church
Mercer Thomas, writer, merlins wynd
Mercer Archibald, baillie Fyfe's clofe
Mercer Mrs, brifto-ftreet
Michie William, merchant, fountain clofe

Michie Thomas, merchant, head of Liberton's wynd
Middlemist Robert, dancing master, bailie Fyfe's cl.
Middlemist Robert, baker, grass market, S. side
Middlemist Mrs, up foot of merlin's wynd
Middleton lady Diana, Nicolson's street
Middleton and Innes, grocers, below Chalmers' close
Millar James, writer, Henderson's stairs
Miller Thomas, writer, bull turnpike
Millar Patrick, banker, bristo street
Millar Mrs, auctioneer, Murdoch's close
Millar Mrs, room letter, Skinner's close
Millar Robert stay-maker, St Mary's wynd
Millars F & M haberdashers, head of Niddrey's w.
Millar John, Esq. advocate, advocate's close
Millar James, musician, Toderick's wynd
Millar Mrs, St Andrew's street
Miller James writer, jun. Skinner's close
Millar John, mathemat. instrument maker, parl. sq.
Millar Mrs, taylor's land, canongate
Millar Arch. coach maker, foot of canongate
Millars Thomas and George, brewers, abbey close
Millar Alexander, advocate, new bank close
Millar Thomas, grocer, Niddrey's wynd
Millar William, merchant, luckenbooths
Millar Miss, merchant, luckenbooths
Millar Alexr. portrait painter, writers court
Millar Mrs, baker, above canongate church
Millar John, gunsmith, head of Chalmers' close
Millar John, silver turner, Libberton's wynd
Millar William, seedsman, horse wynd, canongate
Millar Thomas, silk dyer, lower calton
Millar William, hatter, foot of old assembly close
Millar John, wright, head of the pleasance
Millar Robert, wright, Robertson's close, cowgate
Millar Andrew, wheel wright, fish market close
Millar Alexr, confectioner, Moffat's close, netherb.
Millar Daniel, grocer, head of new street
Millar Robert, grocer, below linen hall
Millar Miss, embroidress, Murdoch's close
Miller William, bookseller, Marlin's wynd
Miller Matthew, inn-keeper, Peeble's wynd
Millar Charles, turner, head of Libberton's wynd

Millar George, merchant, Skinners clofe

Millar James, oppofite Britifh linen hall canongate

Miller James, glover, head of Gray's clofe

Millar George, barber, above canongate church

Millar Andrew, taylor, pleafance

Millar Alexander, glazier, canongate head

Millar James, glover, below bifhop's land

Millar Mrs, midwife, Galloway's clofe

Milligan Andrew, watch-cafe maker, canongate h.

Millians Charles, ftay-maker, flefh market clofe, can.

Mills Thomas, leather merchant, head of new ftreet

Milne James, turner, Boyd's clofe

Milne and Son, iron-mongers, bifhop's land

Milne James, ftocking frame maker, N. back of can

Milne William, grocer, Nicolfon's ftreet

Milne Robert, wright, briffo fireet

Milne James, wheel wright, Leith wynd

Milne Mrs, briffo ftreet

Milne David, merchant, Campbell's ftairs

Milroy Andrew, taylor, new ftreet

Milton lady, canongate foot

Mitcalf Francis, vintner, prefident ftairs

Mitchell Mrs, widow relict of Mr Mitchell, late accomptant of the royal bank, potter-row

Mitchel Alexander, officer of excife, potter-row

Mitchel Alexander, baker, canongate-head

Mitchel Andrew, grocer, Abbey

Mitchel William, French teacher, covenant clofe

Mitchel Mrs, merchant, head of Libberton's wynd

Mitchel Mrs, Kinloch's clofe

Mitchel John, merchant Leith wynd

Mitchel Archibald, faddler, portfburgh

Mitchel George, fhoe maker, blackfriars wynd foot

Mitchel Robert, barber, Alifon's fquare

Mitchell James, vintner, old bank clofe

Mitchell George, fhoe maker, mint

Mitchell William, vintner, flefh market clofe

Mitchell Mrs, calton hill

Mitchell John, officer of exc. taylor's land, canong.

Mitchelfon Sam. fenr. wr. to the fig. Carruber's clofe

Mitchelfon Sam. junr. wr. to the fig. Nicolfon's ftreet

Mitchelfons Miffes, Alifon's fquare

Mitchelson James, lapidary, caftle hill
Moffat Thomas, writer, old bank clofe
Moffat William, fpirit dealer, Kinloch's clofe
Moffat Cumberland, druggift, nether-bow
Moffat Mrs, lint merchant, portfburgh
Moffat George, weaver, portfburgh
Moffat Peter, grocer, brifto ftreet
Moffat James, fhoe-maker, potter-row
Moffat James, wright, crofs-caufey
Moffat Mrs, room-letter, Miln's fquare
Moffat William, writer, Libberton's wynd
Moir James, teacher of languages, Forrefter's wynd
Moir Mrs, John, merchant, at the crofs, north fide
Molliner Charles, glafs blower, Giant's clofe
Molyfon James, fhagreen cafe-maker, Dickfon's clofe
Molyfon Mrs, Forrefter's wynd
Moncrief John writer, Forrefter's wynd
Moncrief David Stewart, advocate, horfe wynd-
Moncrief William, writer, Bell's wynd
Moncrief Mrs, of Fudie, Gairdner's land, canongate
Moncrief John, apothecary, bridge ftreet
Moncrief Sir Henry, minifter, weft church
Moncrief Mifs, gooledub
Moncur Robert, fhoe-maker, oppofite canongate ch.
Moncur Robert, fhoe maker, grafs market
Monro Alex. profeffor of anatomy, &c. Nicolfon's ftr.
Monro John, advocate, Gosford's clofe
Monro Daniel, grocer, fountain well
Monro John, merchant, head of Turk's clofe
Monro Alex. vintner, Borthwick's clofe
Monro George, watch maker, Hyndford's clofe, can.
Monro Richard, weaver, crofs cauley
Monro George, vintner, Byer's clofe
Monro Nicol, fhoe maker, portfburgh
Monro James, fhoe-maker, portfburgh
Monro Rofs, advocate, of Pitcalney Brody's clofe
Monro Drue Jofeph, writer, Buchan's court
Monro William, grocer, canongate head
Monteiths Mifs St John's ftreet
Montieth Mrs, brifto ftreet
Montford Mifs, mantua-maker, Carruber's clofe
Montford and Calder, milliners, Carruber's clofe

Montgomery John Beaumont, of Lamiekan, abbey
Montgomery Lady, abbey hill
Montgomery Mrs, Brifto ftreet
Montgomery James, Efq. general examiner of excife
    horfe wynd, canongate
Montgomery William, wig-maker, oppofite the guard
Montgomery Francis, wig maker, canongate head
Mortgomery Andrew, ftabler, grafs market, S. fide
Montgomery Matthew, writer, Libberton's wynd
Moodie Henry, ftay-maker, fhoe-makers land, can.
Moodie James barber, weft bow
Moodie John, fchool-matter, above the canongate ch.
Moodie Walter, paper-mould-maker, caftle barns
Moodie George, writer, brifto ftreet
Moodie Andrew, grocer, portfburgh
Moodie Mrs, Nicolfon's ftreet
More Mrs, Jack's land, canongate
More, Robert, jeweller, Moffat's clofe
More John, painter, Brown's clofe, luckenbooths
More Andrew, wright, foot of the crofs-caufey
More John, book binder, Brown's clofe, luckenbooths
More John, fmith, Chalmers' clofe
More Mrs, mantua maker, Moffat's clofe
More Patrick, fhoe-maker, Niddry's wynd
More John, writer to the fignet Lady Stairs clofe
More William, ftabler, cowgate head
More James, fchoolmafter, Forrefter's wynd
More and M'Kenzie, fhoe makers, f. of Forreft wynd
More John, beft fowens maker, Dickfon's clofe
More Mrs, Nicolfon's ftreet
More Mrs, Miln's fquare
Morgan J. hair pin & filh hook manuf. op. St. John's ftr
Morgan Henry, grocer, portfburgh
Morgan Thomas, watch maker, head of Bell's wynd
Morice George, hair dreffer, front of James' court
Morifon William, writer, Brown's fquare
Morrfon Anftruther, Efq. Megat's land, weft port
Morifon James, principal clerk, annexed eftates office
    middle of Leith walk
Morrifon   , limner, Tweedale's clofe
Morifon Mifs back of the fountain well
Morifon Mifs, St John's ftreet

Morifon John, writer of excife, calton
Morifon Hugh, officer of excife, caftle wynd
Morifon Alex. notary and meffenger, Warrifton's cl.
Morifon, M'Gowan, and Co. miliners, luckenbooths
Morifon Alexander, hatter, parliament houfe
Morifon Robert, fhoe-maker, St Mary's wynd
Morifon Robert, fhoe-maker, head of the pleafance
Morifon Alexander, plaifterer, wrights houfes
Morifon Mrs, room fetter, Niddrey's wynd
Morifon Hugh, hair dreffer, Brifto-ftreet
Morifon Mrs, room-letter, back of canongate
Morifon William, cuftom houfe of Leith, Leith walk
Morifon Mrs, Baron Grant's clofe
Morris Robert, wright, nether bow
Morris Alexander, ftabler, cowgate head
Mortimer Robert, breeches-maker, canongate
Mortimer George, breeches-maker, brifto-ftreet
Morton Walter, writing mafter, accomptant of excife
    oppofite the guard
Morton Robert, writer, advocates clofe
Morton John, writing-mafter, Cant's clofe
Morton David, brewer, bunker's hill
Morton John, fhoe-maker, brifto-ftreet
Morton Robert fhoe-maker, above Queenfberry lodg.
Mofses John, fpirit dealer, cowgate head
Mofsman Hugh, writer to the fignet, Stodart's cl. cow.
Mofman John, merchant, lawn market
Moubray Chriftopher, oppofite foot of Niddery's wy.
Moubray Mrs, Toderick's wynd
Moubray Mrs, St Andrew's ftreet
Moubray Robert, haberdafher, oppofite Alifon's fquare
Moubray Martin, clerk in the poft office, Wardrope's c.
Moubray Alex. merchant, Caitchen's land cowgate
Moubray William, hair-merchant, back of the guard
Moubray John, hair-merchant, Middleton's entry
Moubray and Adams Mifes, Allifon's clofe, cowgate h
Mounfay John, of Rammerfcales, Efq college wynd
Moyfe, minifter, oppofite the new chapel
Moyfe Shadrach, Efq; St Andrew's ftreet
Moyfe Robert, flefher, flefh-market clofe
Moyfe Thomas, tayler, grafs market north fide

K

Muat Mrs, Miln's square
Muat and Aitken, merchants, Dickson's close
Muat James, writing-master, Dickson's close
Mugerland Andrew, cooper, canongate foot
Munro Miss Trunk close
Munro James, grocer, horse wynd
Munro William, vintner, luckenbooths
Munro William, merchant, calton hill
Munro William, musician, Peeble's wynd
Muir Mrs, abbey-hill
Muir George, writer to the signet, Brown's square
Muir William, stabler, grass market N. side
Muirhead William, smith, calton
Muirhead William, brush-maker, lawn market
Murdoch George, stabler, grass market S. side
Murdoch Andrew, mason, Richmond street
Murdoch Malcom, grocer, St Andrew's street
Murdoch James, wheel-wright, Stonelaw's close
Murdoch Thomas, stone ware merchant, Peeble's w.
Murison Andrew, writer, bailie Fyfe's close
Murison Peter, taylor, James' court
Murray Walter, writer, Patterson's court
Murray Mrs, of Stormonth, baillie Fyfe's close
Murray Mrs, of Cringeltie, south Gray's close
Murray Mrs, of Balmanno, Henderson's stairs
Murray the Earl of, chapel street
Murray Mrs, Farm's land, west bow foot
Murray Alexander, advocate, Argyle's square
Murray Patrick, advocate, Kincaid's land, cowgate
Murray David, writer, castle hill
Murray and Cochran, printers, Craig's close
Murray Mungo, stabler, cowgate head
Murray James stabler, head of the pleasance
Murray William, haberdasher, canongate head,
Murray Duncan, merchant, op. blackfriar's wynd
Murray James, merchant, head of Toderick's wynd
Murray John, merchant, luckenbooths
Murray Robert, wool merc. Blyth's close, castle hill
Murray Andrew, grocer, grass market, north side
Murray William, grocer, head of St John's street
Murray David, grocer, foot of Forrester's wynd
Murray James, grocer, back of the city guard

Murray Daniel, grocer, cowgate head
Murray Adam, baxter, front of James' court
Murray John, smith, shoe maker's close, canongate
Murray John, baxter, head of James's court
Murray Adam, wright, crofs-caufey
Murray James, taylor, Leith wynd
Murray William, shoemaker, exchange
Murray Robert, shoemaker, canongate head
Murray Robert, shoemaker, portsburgh
Murray and M'Harg, tobacconifts, below flesh m. cl.
Murray Andrew, barber, luckenbooths
Murray Mifs, mantua maker, Henderson's stairs
Murray William of Polmaife, shoemaker's close, can.
Murray Hen. ladies hair dreff. head of bailie Fyfe's cl.
Murray Adam, turner and hard ware mer. bridge ftr.
Murray Will. writer, St Mary's wynd
Murray George, writer, calton hill
Murray William, writer, Galloway's cl. lawn mark.
Murray James, writer, Warden's close, grafs-mark.
Murray Mrs, keeps boarders, Niddery's wynd
Murray Mrs, room setter, flesh market close
Murray J. printer and auctioneer, parliament square
Murray David, room setter, Kennedy's close
Murray Mrs, room setter, advocate's close
Murray Mrs, room-setter, Cooper's land canongate
Murray Admiral, Carrubber's close
Murray Will. wr. at Mrs M'Hattie's Wardrope's court
Murray Mrs, Cant's close
Murray Alexander, printer, Marlin's wynd
Murray Adam, grocer, foot of Forrefter's wynd
Murray Mrs, chaple street
Murray Patrick, baxter, crofs caufey
Murray William, baxter, cowgate-head
Murray James, grocer, horfe wynd
Mufhet George, mufician, Toderick's wynd
Mufhet Mifs, mantua maker, weft bow
Mutter Mrs, canongate head
Mutter Thomas, merchant, Gavinloch's land
Mutter Mifs, oppofite lady Milton's lodging
Myrtles Mifs, oppofite chapel of Eafe

N

Nairn William, advocate, Argyle's square

Nairn Captain Thomas, new ftreet, canongate
Nairn Mrs, fouth Gray's clofe
Nairn John, merchant, head of Libberton's wynd
Nairns Robert and Adam, barbers, canongate head
Nairn William, grocer, head of Kinloch's clofe
Nairn Alexander, writer, St Andrew's fquare
Napier the hon. Captain Charles, George's fquare
Napier Archibald, druggift, head of Forrefter's wynd
Napier Alexander, mufician, foot of Bell's wynd
Napier Honourable Mrs, St Agnes ftreet
Nafmith Michael, wright, fhop, new ftreet, canong.
    houfe, Miln's land, canongate
Nafmith Robert, Efq, potter-row
Nafmith Mifles, South Gray's clofe
Nafmith Mrs, potter-row
Neal John, merchant, back of the guard
Neil Thomas, wright, luckenbooths
Neill and Co. printers, old fifh market clofe
Neill Adam, printer, foot of Forrefter's wynd
Neilfon Mrs, of Corfack, calton hill
Neilfon James, hair dreffer, head of Chalmers' clofe
Neilfon Andrew, room letter, college wynd
Neilfon Thomas, head of Young's ftreet
Neilfon John, Campbell's clofe, canongate
Neilfon James, hair-dreffer, St Mary's wynd
Neilfon George, Efq, St David's ftreet
Newton George, baker, pleafance
Newton and Morifon, milliners, oppofite the guard
Niblie Archibald, writer to the fignet, caftle hill
Nicol William, watch-maker, head of Bell's wynd
Nicol Robert and Co. hatters, Bever-hall
Nicol Wil. one of the highfchool mafters, Richmond ft.
Nicol David, fmith, pleafance
Nicolfon Alexander, plumber, caftle hill
Nicolfons Mifs, milliners, back of the guard
Nicolfon James, barber, St Ninian's row
Nimmo William, fupervifor, Alifon's fquare
Nimmo Peter and James, brewers, potter row
Nimmo John, barber, cowgate head
Nimmo Thomas, baker, Charles' ftreet
Nimmo James, barber, cowgate-head
Nifbet lady, of Dean, Nicolfon's ftreet

Nisbet William, linen manufacturer, potter-row port
Nisbet Alexander, merchant, lawn market, north-side
Nisbet David, merchant, abbey
Nisbet Mrs, victualler, foot of college wynd
Nisbet Mrs, of Dean, Alison's close cowgate-head
Noble Robert, eastmost meal market stairs
Noble and Stevenson, grocers, cross causey
Noble William, schoolmaster, flesh-market close, can.
Noble John, spirit dealer, cowgate-head
Norrie Mrs, painter, head of Morison's close
Norrie Mrs, grocer, canongate-head
Norris Joseph, writer, bow foot
Norvell George, of Boghall, Esq, new town
Noteman John, candle-maker, canongate-head

O

Oatts Charles, shoe-maker, bridge-street
Ochiltree Archibald, goldsmith, anchor close
Ogg John, stabler, bristo street
Ogilvie Adam, advocate, Carrubber's close
Ogilvie James, custom-house
Ogilvie George, advocate, back stairs
Ogilvie Duncan, schoolmaster, Kinloch's close
Ogilvie Malcolm, Cleland's yards
Ogilvie David, St Mary's wynd
Ogilvie James, shoe maker, Leith wynd
Ogilvie Alexander, glover, head of Carruber's close
Ogilvie Thomas, writer, Miln's court
Ogilvie James, writer, Peebles wynd
Oliver Mrs, Richmond street
Ogle John, writer, castle wynd
Ogle Alan, wright, canongate head
Oliphant Robert, post mast. gen. shoe makers cl. can.
Oliphant Mrs room setter, Nicolson's street
Oliphant Mrs, fountain close
Oliphant Charles, perfumer, head of bailie Fyfe's cl.
Oliphant Ebenezer, goldsmith, Forrester's wynd
Orme David, writer, Stonelaw's close
Orme Alexander, principal clerk of session, Miln's sq.
Ormiston Mrs, Forrester's wynd
Ormiston Miss, Nicolson's street
Ormiston John, mason, Bruce's close, grass market
Orr Mrs, Miln's court

Orr Mrs, grafs-market
Orr John, ſtocking-maker, Richmond ſtreet
Orrock Alexander, grocer, foot of Forreſter's wynd
Orrock John, cutler, head of Barrenger's cloſe
Orrocks Miſs, mantua makers, ſociey port
Oſburn Alexander, writer, bull turnpike
Oſwald Andrew, grocer, north back of canongate
Oſwald Mrs, room-ſetter, north Gray's cloſe

P

Paſley Ninian, merchant, Briſto ſtreet
Palmer Alexander, wright, chapel ſtreet
Panton Mrs, croſs cauſey
Park John, ſhoe-maker, fleſh-market cloſe, canongate
Parlane James, ſpirit dealer, foot of Forreſters wynd
Paſquali Mrs, oppoſite linen hall canongate
Paterſon Mrs, bailie Fyfe's cloſe
Paterſon Miſs oppoſite linen hall
Paterſon John, architect, St John's ſtreet
Paterſon William, ſtabler, kings ſtables
Paterſon David, printer, lawn market
Paterſon Samuel, merchant, luckenbooths
Paterſon Mrs, room-ſetter, covenant cloſe
Paterſon John, taylor, Turk's cloſe
Paterſon James, taylor, Morrocco's cloſe
Paterſon Miſs, mantua maker, old aſſembly cloſe
Paterſon John, ſhoe maker, portſburgh
Paterſon Robert, ſhoe maker, croſs cauſey
Paterſon James, cork cutter, op foot of Niddery's wy,
Patterſon Miſs, oppoſite linen hall
Patterſon James, baxter, briſto-ſtreet
Patterſon Thomas, taylor, canal ſtreet
Patterſon Miſs, cowgate-head
Patterſon William, confectioner, portſburgh
Patterſon Mrs, mantua-maker, portſburgh
Patterſon John, ſtabler, grafs-market
Paton Robert, writer,
Paton James, limner, oppoſite foot of Niddery's wy,
Paton George, of the cuſtoms, caſtle-hill
Paton Miſs, milliner, caſtle hill
Paton George, book-binder, Con's cloſe
Pattiſon John, miniſter, briſto-ſtreet
Pattullo Mrs, Foulis' cloſe

Pattullo and Blair, milliners at the crofs, north fide

Patullo Mrs, uppermoft Jack's clofe

Paxton James, coach-maker, new inn grafs market

Peacock Thomas, painter, foot of new ftreet

Pearfon Mrs, Caitchen's land, cowgate

Pearfon Adam, clerk, oppofite the Britifh linen hall

Peat John, writer, Byers' clofe

Peat Allan, taylor, baillie Fyfe's clofe

Peat Alexander, fupervifor of excife op. Linen hall

Penman George, fhoe-maker, Libberton's wynd

Pentland John, turner weft bow

Pender Thomas, ftamp-office

Peterkin and Son, taylors, pleafance

Peter Gabriel, baillie Fyfe's clofe

Peter William taylor, new ftreet, canongate

Peters Mrs, taylor, St Andrew's ftreet

Petrie William, fhoe-maker, canongate foot

Pettygrew John, watch-maker, weft port

Pew William, baxter, oppofite Milton's lodging

Philipe Richard-Alifon, writer, St John's ftreet

Philipe William, turner, brifto-ftreet

Philipe Thomas, print-feller, foot of horfe wynd

Philipe Robert, wright, Buccleugh's ftreet

Philiphaugh Lady, George's fquare

Philip James, judge-admiral, Craig's clofe

Philip Mrs, milliner, Roxburgh's clofe

Philip John, fhoe-maker, canongate-foot

Phin and Pattifon, haberdafhers, op. blackfriars wy

Phin William, filk-dyer, caftle-hill

Picque, dancing-mafter, fkinners clofe

Pillans John, brewer, caftle wynd

Pillans M. and E. milliners, head of Dickfon's clofe

Pillans Robert, brewer, head of Wardrope's court

Pine Mrs, fkinner's clofe

Pine Miffes, milliner, Skinners clofe

Pinkerton Francis, writer, Robertfen's clofe, cowgate

Pirney William, mafon, calton-hill

Pirrie Alex extractor, M'Kenzie's office, parl. fquare

Pirrie James, writer, Nairn's clofe

Pirrie George, merchant, head of advocate's clofe

Purie William, taylor, head of new ftreet

Purie William, ftay maker Semple's clofe

Pirrie John, hair-merchant, Peeble's wynd
Pitcairn Mrs, Campbell's land, canongate
Pitcairn Andrew, sen. writer, Halkerston's wynd
Pitcairn Andrew, jun. writer, bull turnpike
Pitcairn Captain George, Fowlis' clofe
Pitcairn James, wright, grafs-market, fouth fide
Pitfour Lady, caufey fide
Playfair Robert, writer, fociety
Plenderleith David, minifter, Gabriel's road
Plenderleith Alexander, taylor, Chrichton's ftreet
Pleydell Mrs, potter row
Plumber Andrew, advocate, Argyle's fquare
Pollock John grocer, head of Niddery's wynd
Pollock John ftabler, cowgate-head
Pollock William, fmith, at the canongate church
Polton William, merchant, head of horfe-wynd
Ponton Mifs, merchants, luckenbooths
Ponton Alexander, wright, canal ftreet
Poole Matthew, keeper of Pince's ftreet coffee-houfe
Porteous David, painter, at the tron church
Porteous James, mafon, brifto-ftreet
Porteous Alexander, flefher, flefh market clofe
Porteous James, book binder, Nicolfon's ftreet
Porteous David, taylor, high fchool wynd
Porteous Mis, room-fetter, cowgate-head
Porteous James, clerk, Miln's court
Porterfield Mrs, Ramfay garden caftle-hill
Potts Thomas, grocer, candle-maker row
Potts George, wright, head of the pleafance
Powfowls lady, Charles' ftreet
Piatt George, taylor, portfburgh
Prefton Miffes, Riddle's land
Preftons Mifs, of Valleyfield, Hyndford's clofe
Pridie Hampden, hatter, St Mary's wynd
Pridie David, hatter, head of new ftreet
Primrofe Robert, furgeon, head of Toderick's wynd
Primrofe Mifs, chaple-ftreet
Primrofe Mifs, Hyndford's clofe,
Pringle Robert, of Symington, coats-hall
Pringle John, of Crichton, George fquare
Pringle William, taylor, Richmond ftreet
Pringle Mrs, new ftreet, canongate

Pringle Mrs, blackfriars wynd
Pringle John, advocate, blackfriars wynd
Pringle John, writer to the signet, society
Pringle Dunbar, tanner, canon mills
Pringle John, dancing-master, blackfriars wynd
Pringle John, officer of exc grafs market, north side
Pringle Mifs, milliner, front of the exchange
Pringle James, wright, portfburgh
Pringle John, yarn boiler, Niddery's wynd
Pringle Mrs, of Bowland, old affembly clofe
Pringle Mifs, Miln's court
Pringle George, of Torritlee,
Pringle Mrs, of Lochton, Crichton ftreet
Pringle Mifs, George's fquare
Pringle Mrs, of Whitebank, Nicolfon's ftreet
Pringle Mrs, vintner, parliament fquare
Profit Mrs, Middleton's entry
Profit James, taylor, abbey ftrand
Puppo Jofeph, mufician, Young's ftreet
Puppo Stephane, teacher of languages, James' court
Purdie Thomas, at the charity work-h. crofs caufey
Purfell William, fmith, Haftie's clofe, cowgate
Purves Alexander, merchant, Reid's clofe, canong.
Purves Thomas, vintner prefident ftairs
Purves James, ftabler, horfe-wynd
Pym Jofeph, haberdafher, bridge ftreet

R

Rae lady, St John's ftreet
Rae lady, Crichton ftreet
Rae David, advocate, old affembly clofe
Rae James, furgeon, caftle hill
Rae James procurator, foot of advocates clofe
Rae John, merchant, grafs market, north fide
Rae George, upholfterer, Leith wynd
Rae Mifs mantua-maker, head of Bell's wynd
Rae George, hook maker, Leith wynd
Rae William, taylor, Toderick's wynd
Raeburn Wil ladies hair-dreffer and perf bridge ftr.
Ralph Alexander, ftabler, grafs market
Ramage James, old bank, oppofite Milton's lodging
Ramidge William, tea and fpirit dealer, portfburgh

L

Ramidge James, tea dealer, weſt-bow head
Ramidge John, ſhoemaker, two penny cuſtom
Ramidge Patrick, barber, Buccleugh's ſtreet
Ramidge Edward, St David's ſtreet, new town
Ramſay Mrs, lochend's cloſe, canongate
Ramſay Robert, phyſician George's ſquare
Ramſay John, advocate, Carrubber's cloſe
Ramſay William, writer, Carrubber's cloſe
Ramſay James, accomptant, weſt end of lauriſton
Ramſay Martin, writer, canongate head
Ramſay David, maſon, Shakeſpeare's ſquare
Ramſay Robert, taylor, Gray's cloſe
Ramſay Peter, ſtabler, cowgate port
Ramſay James, builder, new ſtreet, canongate
Ramſay James, trunk maker, lawn market, N. ſide
Ramſay, George, ſmith, entry to Nicolſon's ſtreet
Ramſay William, ſhoemaker, pleaſance
Ramſay Mrs, libberton's wynd
Ramſay James, painter, horſe wynd
Ramſay John, wright, Paul's work
Ranken James, lapidary, Morocco's cloſe
Ranken James, wright, Fowlis' cloſe
Ranken William, dyer, op. the foot of horſe wynd
Ranken William, ſen taylor, croſs cauſey
Ranken William, jun. taylor, luckenbooths
Ranken George, merchant, bridge ſtreet
Ranken James, rum merchant, graſs market
Rankens Staffordſhire ſtone-ware-houſe, bridge ſtreet
Rannie Thomas, writer, back of the guard
Rannie Mr, ſetts rooms, cowgate head
Rannie and Campbell, merchants, front of exchange
Rannie John, baxter, abbey ſtrand
Rannie Mrs, mantua-maker, Forreſter's wynd
Rattray Thomas, writer, Carrubber's cloſe
Rattray James, brewer, oppoſite new ſtairs cowg.
Rattray Miſs, mantua-maker, fiſh market cloſe
Rattray Peter, grocer, water gate
Reddie James, maſon, Leith wynd
Reid George, printer, Fiſher's land cloſe, lawn-market
     vender of all Dr Hill's and other valuable medicines
Reid James, miniſter, St John's ſtreet
Reid Matth. plumber, Currie's cloſe, graſs market

Reid James, and Co. linen printers, at Gorgie
Reid Alexander, jeweller, parliament square
Reid John writer, advocates clofe
Reid Mrs, iron monger, op. the guard
Reid Walter, weaver, Paul's work
Reid Mrs, fountain clofe
Reid Patrick, upholfterer, baron Maule's clofe
Reid James, manufacturer, Gifford's park, fcinnes
Reid Lawrence, wright, abbey-hill
Reid Alexander, grocer, head of Forrefter's wynd
Reid James, grocer, head of the pleafance
Reid William, tobbaconift, mid flefh market clofe
Reid William, ftocking maker, foot of the college w.
Reid Andrew, barber, St Ninian's row
Reid Thomas, room fetter, flefh market clofe
Reid John, grocer, new-inn, grafs market
Reid Alexander, mafon, Forrefter's wynd
Reid Mrs, feamftrefs, Libberton's wynd
Reid Charles, baker, at the crofs
Reid James, grocer, nether bow
Reid Thomas, baker, Leith wynd
Reikie James, glazier, Miln's fquare
Reikie Thomas, glazier, old fifh market clofe
Reinagle Jofeph, mufician, Blackfriars wynd
Renton Robert, writer, head of James's court
Renton Mrs, oppofite bow head well
Reoch James, procurator, Murdoch's clofe
Reoch William, cabinet maker, Carrubber's clofe
Reoch John, mufician, fouth end of the theatre
Reoch Charles, Balfour's coffee-houfe
Reynolds Mis, room fetter, Miln's fquare
Rhind William, copper-fmith, welt bow foot
Rhind Charles, eaft end of crofs caufey
Rhind John, writer, Dalrymple's office
Richardfon William, procurator, Borthwick's clofe
Richardfon Robert, writer, at the linen hall
Richardfon Richard, grocer, exchange
Richardfons Mifs, milliners, head of Swan's clofe
Richardfon James, flater, Jack's clofe, canongate
Richardfon Adam, fhoemaker, St Mary's wynd
Richardfon William, hat-drefler, Chalmers' clofe

Richardson Mrs, room setter, op new chapel, cowg.
Richardson Robert, founder, St Ninian's row
Richardson William, smith, Wright's close, cowgate
Richardson Will. jun. smith, new chapel, cowg
Richardson William, merchant, Forrester's wynd
Richmond Misses, mantua-maker, old flesh market close
Richmond James, land surveyor, gr. market, S. side
Richmond John seedsman, west bow foot
Riddell James, Esq, St John's street
Riddell Mrs, of Mauselay, chapel street
Riddell Miss, St Andrew's street
Riddell Mrs, bristo street
Riddell William, writer to the signet, teviot row
Riddell James, smith, new street
Riddle Colonel, George's square
Riddoch John, white-iron smith, west bow head
Rigg Thomas, Esq, Gostord's close
Rigg James-Home, of Gamelshiells, Fisher's close
Rigg George, Turk's close
Ritchie Alexander, merchant, lawn market, N. side
Ritchies Miss, milliners, front of the exchange
Ritchie and Crichton, smiths, newington
Ritchie Mrs, candle maker, horse wynd, canongate
Ritchie Thomas, wright, back of St Ninian's row
Ritchie Miss, room setter, Dickson's close
Ritter Joseph, grocer, bow-head
Rob Mrs, prince's street
Rob Mrs, keeps lodgers, potter-row
Rob Mrs, north Gray's close
Robb Andrew, merchant, grass market
Robb John, merchant, foot of candle-maker-row
Robb and Hutchison, merchants, luckenbooths
Robbs Miss, mantua makers, potter-row
Robertson Alexander, vintner, Kennedy's close
Robertson John, fleet custom, old fish market close
Robertson Miss, west bow foot
Robertson Roger, of Ladykirk, Newhall house potter-r
Robertson Alexander, hair-dresser, Kincaid's land
Robertson Mrs, Nicolson's street
Robertson John, grocer, bristo street
Robertson Mrs, canal street

Robertson David, Efq; George's fquare

Robertson John, printer of Caledonian **Mercury**, back ftairs.——Houfe laurieston

Robertson Hugh, turner, caftle-hill

Robertson James, flesher, flesh-market clofe

Robertson Dundas, furgeon, end of brifto-ftreet

Robertson John, profeffor, brifto port

Robertson Walter, weft end of laurifton

Robertson Jofeph, furgeon, bifhops land

Robertson William, principal, college

Robertson James profeffor, college

Robertson Alex. principal clerk of feffion, Miln's fquare

Robertson Barclay-James, wr to the fig St John's ftr.

Robertson William, writer, Prince's ftreet

Robertson John, writer, Carrubber's clofe

Robertson William, writer, old affembly clofe

Robertson Charles, writer, Borthwick's clofe

Robertson John, writer, meal-market ftairs

Robertson John, clofet-keeper, Chalmers' clofe

Robertson Robert, architect, St Andrew's ftreet

Robertson Alexander, printer, Niddery's wynd

Robertson Patrick, jeweller, parliament fquare

Robertson William, watch-maker, canongate head

Robertson John, gold-fmith, above new ftreet, can.

Robertson William, limner, old play houfe clofe

Robertson Charles, painter, prince's ftreet

Robertson Geo. defigner in gardening, Princes ftreet

Robertson Peter, merchant, front of exchange

Robertson Charles, hard ware merchant, lawn market

Robertson John, fen flesher, flesh-market clofe

Robertson James, ftabler, pleafance

Robertson David fmith, cowgate head

Robertson Hugh, ftay and habit maker, Leith wynd

Robertson James, grocer, canongate foot

Robertson James, grocer, cowgate head

Robertson Richard, baxter, foot of the pleafance

Robertson William, dyer, water of Leith

Robertson William, grocer, head of Marquis of Tweed-dale's clofe

Robertson William, writer, Paterfon's court

Robertson Thomas, timber-merchant, goofe-dub

Robertson James, grocer, Nicolfon's ftreet

Robertson David, baker, Leith wynd
Robertson Agnes, lint-dresser, Stonelaw's close
Robertson James, shoe maker, potter-row
Robertson John, barber, opposite fountain well
Robertson John, barber, west port
Robertson John, barber, foot of Niddery's wynd
Robertson Alexander, vintner, Gosford's cl. lawn-mar.
Robertson David, glover, castle hill north side
Robertson Joseph, minister, canal street
Robertson Robert, candlemaker, Kincaid's land, cow.
Robertson Mrs, milliner, prince's street
Robertson Miss, mantua-maker, Tod's cl. castle hill
Robertson John, stay and habit maker, canong. head
Roberts William, physician, Sommer-hall
Roberts Mrs, hoop-maker, baron Grants close
Roche Mrs, bunkers hill
Rocheid of Inverleith, Esq; St John's street
Rodgers Hugh, cork cutter, opposite St John's street
Rodgers George, cork-cutter, abbey strand
Rodgers James, grocer, west port
Rolland Adam, advocate, exchange
Rollo Robert, grocer, lawn market
Rollo Andrew, cooper, canongate foot
Rollo Miss, Hanover street
Romainous William, stocking-maker, castle-hill
Ronaldson William, baker, lawn market, south side
Ronaldson James, shoe-maker, foot of college wynd
Ronaldson John, grocer, head of south Gray's close
Ronaldson Mrs, canongate foot
Ronaldson Allan, canongate foot
Ronaldson Andrew, of Blair hall, below Crichton's entry
Ronaldson Francis, bristo-street
Rose John, schoolmaster, Leith wynd
Rose Mrs, of Leith, foot of new street
Ross Mrs, of Invernethie, Campbell's land
Ross Mrs, of Pitcalney, Brodie's close, lawn-market
Ross of Balingown Captain, George's square
Ross David, cook, South Gray's close
Ross Patrick, musician, Toderick's wynd
Ross Mrs, Buccleugh street
Ross Walter, writer to the signet, meal market stairs
Ross Matthew, advocate, castle hill

Rofs Alexander, dep. clerk of feffion caftle hill
Rofs Robert, mufic fhop, back of the fountain well
Rofs Mifs milliner head of old affembly clofe
Rofe Patrick, wright, Morteith's clofe
Rofs David, accomptant, bull turnpike
Rofs Robert, teacher of mathematics, Bell's wynd
Rofs Colin, macer in exchequer, new ftreet
Rofs Donald, candle maker, portfburgh
Rofs Mrs, room fetter, Buchanan's court
Rofs Alexander, merchant, grafs market
Rough William, fhoemaker, portfburgh
Roupel Mrs, Somervell's clofe, canongate
Rowley Mifs, new ftreet
Ruddiman Walter, and Thos printers, Forrefter's w.
Rue William, writer, Toderick's wynd
Rule Alexr. taylor, flefh market clofe, canongate
Rule Thomas, writer, Roxburgh's clofe
Rule George, baker, St Andrew's ftreet
Runciman Alexander, painter, foot of the pleafance
Ruffel Mrs, Afshiltill, brifto ftreet
Ruffel James, writer, city clerk's office
Ruffel James, furgeon, fociety
Ruffel Thomas, grocer, canongate-head
Ruffel Henry, Hyndford's clofe
Ruffel John, fenr. writer to the fig, Argyle's fq.
Ruffel John, junr. writer, Argyle's fq.
Ruffel David, accomptant, fociety,
Ruffel James, upholfterer, bailhe Fyfe's clofe
Ruffel Robert and Son, merchants, luckenbooths
Ruffel John, wright, portfburgh
Ruffel James, taylor, St Mary's wynd
Rutherford James, Efq, old affembly clofe
Rutherford Henry, Hunthill, Efq, mint court
Rutherford Mrs, Crichton's ftreet
Rutherford Mrs, of Fardingtown, brifto-ftreet
Rutherford James, writer, old affembly clofe
Rutherford George, junr. old affembly clofe
Rutherford Edw. writer to the fig. weft bow foot
Rutherford John, of Edgerftone, George's fquare
Rutherford John, phyfician, Hyndford's clofe
Rutherford David, baxter, grafs market fouth fide,
Rutherford Archibald, drawing mafter, Allan's clofe

Rutherford John, advocate, George's square
Rutherford James, furgeon, Nicolfon's ftreet
Rutherford lady, Ahfon's square
Rutherford William, taylor, op. the mint
Ruthven Thomas, writer, plainftone clofe, canong.
Rymer James, engraver, luckenbooths
Rymer Gavin, regifter office for fervants St Mary's wy.

S

Saat Peter, fugar baker, oppofite canongate church
Salifburgh James, architect, bunkers hill
Salter Ifaac, brewer, college wynd
Salton Mrs, glazier, grafs market, fouth fide
Salton Alexander, taylor, weft bow foot
Sampfon David, Blyth's clofe, caftle hill
Samuel John, officer of excife, Monteith's clofe
Sanders John, teller in the royal bank, twopenny cuft.
Sanders James, writer to the fignet, caftle hill
Sanders John, fhoemaker, near the theatre
Sanderfon Thomas, merchant, caftle hill
Sands William, writer, upper baxter's clofe
Sands Mrs, Gabriel's road
Sandilands Mrs, caftle hill
Sandilands Matth writer to the fig. St Andrew's fq.
Sandfide lady, head of flefh market clofe
Sandy George, under keeper to the fignet, new ftairs
Sangfter Peter, book binder, back of the fountain w.
Sangfter James, grocer, potter-row
Sanfon James, grocer, Lochend's clofe canongate
Savage Robert, wig maker, Ahfon's fquare
Sawers William, merchant, head of Turk's clofe
Sawers Archibald, baxter, Forrefter's wynd
Saxan Mrs, room-fetter, potter-row
Schetky George, mufician, Miln's court
Schetman Charles, mufician, Niddery's wynd
Scott and Drummond, milliners, parliament fquare
Scott William, vintner, advocates clofe
Scott Robert, grocer, op. foot of Libberton's wynd
Scott Mrs, pleafance
Scott Mrs, Charles' ftreet
Scott Francis, Efq, George's fquare
Scott Thomas, painter, Duncan's clofe
Scott Walter, of Halden, St Andrew's fquare

Scott William, spirit-dealer, Nicolson's street
Scott Thomas, of Hopsburn, grange
Scott George, writer, back of the guard
Scott James, Esq. writer to the signet, Bess wynd
Scott James, junr. merchant, op the corn market
Scott Miss, of Thirleston, George's square
Scott Miss, of Harden, teviot row
Scott Mrs, of Horshe hill, St Andrew's square
Scott Mis, Alison's square
Scott William, merchant, old assembly close
Scott John, advocate, writers court
Scott William, procurator, Somervell's land, grass m.
Scott Thomas, writer, writers court
Scott John, flesher, high school yards
Scott David, shoe-maker, lower calton
Scott Walter, writer to the signet, George's square
Scott Elias, perfumer, opposite the tron church
Scott William, plumber, Shakespeare square
Scott Archibald, brewer, Potter-row
Scott Alexander, brewer, fountain bridge
Scott David, painter, Duncan's land canongate
Scott John, druggist, near the infirmary
Scott Alexander, merchant, Alison's square
Scott Charles tanner, grass-market, South side
Scott Mrs, of Galla, Robertson's close
Scott John, clerk excise office, siennes
Scott John, grocer, below the fountain well
Scott Walter, merchant, grass market south side
Scott Robert, merchant, head of Swan's close
Scott-Moncrieff Robert, merchant, St Andrew's street
Scott Charles, hair-dresser, luckenbooths
Scott James, iron monger, west bow foot
Scott Henry, carpet manufacturer, pleasance
Scott Thomas, stabler, cowgate-head
Scott James, book-binder, head of Bell's wynd
Scott Robert, grocer, potter-row
Scott James, gun-smith, above Crichton's entry canon.
Scott Miss, mantua-maker, blackfriars wynd
Scott James, tobbacconist, portsburgh
Scott Robert, taylor, Monteith's close

M

Scott Walter, shoe-maker, potter-row

Scott William, shoe-maker, flesh market close can.

Scott Robert, clerk to new english chapel cowgate port

Scott William, writing-master, Dickson's close

Scotland William, officer of excise, new street

Scotland Adam, grocer, foot of college wynd

Scotland William, writer, laurieston

Scotland William, wool-merchant, west bow head

Scrymgeour Alexander, advocate, old assembly close

Scrymgeour James, Warriston's close

Scrymgeour John, grocer, Adams' court

Scyth Robert, upholstery and cabinet ware house, 1st stair below bridge street, dwelling house and work shop Cant's close

Sealy Joseph, dancing master, Foulis' close

Selby Robert, plumber, bailie Fyfe's close

Selkirk Earl of, St John's street

Selkirk Robert, teller in roy. bank, new inn grass m.

Selkrig Mrs, milliner, lawn market, north side

Selkrig Charles, writer, grass market

Sellars Peter, taylor, Leith wynd

Sellar Thomas, foot of Kinloch's close

Sellers Miss, Riddle's land

Sempill John, writer, foot of Stonelaws close

Sempill Miss, Adams' court

Sempill Robert, brewer, castlebarns

Seton Sir Hugh. of Touch, Esq. Chessels' court

Seton John, limner, thistle court

Seton Alexander, brewer, Robertson's close cowgate

Seton, Houston and Co. bankers, exchange

Seton Daniel, merchant, exchange

Seton Robert, barber, abbey strand

Seton Mrs. horse wynd

Seton Mrs, keeps boarders, bristo street

Seton Walter, exchange

Seton and M'Culloch, silk manufactorers, M'Vicar's entry potter-row

Shade Thomas, baker, foot of the cross causey

Shand Francis, merchant, society

Sharp Fran coach-master op. Richmond str. pleasance

Sharp Thomas, secretary, to royal bank, broughton

Sharp John, horfe hyrer, pleafance

Sharp Mrs, pleafance

Sharp Mrs, wind mill ftreet

Shaw Mrs, caftle-hill

Shaw Alexander, wright, St Ninian's row

Shaw Samuel, writer, Warrifton's clofe

Shaw Doctor, Nicolfon's ftreet

Shaw James, procurator, Wardrope's court

Shaw Mifs, new town

Shaw James, grocer, head of St John's ftreet

Schaw George, wine-merchant, calton hill

Shean Chriftian, harpficord and fpinet-maker, new ftr.

Sheppard David, grocer, head of Strichan's clofe

Shiels Archibald, Efq, Swan's clofe

Shiels John, britifh laboratory, at iron church

Shiels Mrs, weft bow

Shiels Francis, baxter, head of Cant's clofe

Shiels Mrs, midwife, caftle-hill

Sheils Mifs, Nairn's clofe

Sherwood Benjamin, fnuff grinder, beaver hall]

Shiriflaw James, grocer, nether-bow

Short Thomas, optician, top of the calton hill

Shortreid Mrs, Aitken's land canongate

Sibbald John, fmith, grafs market fouth fide

Sibbald William, taylor, Brodie's clofe

Sibbald Thomas, fmith, college wynd

Sibbald James, fhoe-maker, oppofite Alifon's fquare

Sime James, of Northfield, Monteith's clofe

Sime Andrew, baker, portfburgh

Sime R. jun writer to fignet, h. of Forrefter's wynd

Sime John, writer to fignet, new ftreet canongate

Sime James, writer, Peebles wynd

Sime Henry, baxter, portfburgh

Sime George, flater, Dickfon's clofe

Sime James, glover, creams

Sime Mrs, St Andrew's fquare

Simpfon James, hair-dreffer, canongate

Simpfon Mrs, head of Blyth's clofe

Simpfon William, cafhier royal bank, new bank clofe

Simpfon Thomas, pewterer, head of bridge ftreet

Simfon James, baxter, op. foot of old fifh market cl.

Simpson Alexander, writer, Bell's wynd
Simpson Mrs, Jack's land, canongate
Simpson Richard, grocer, Anderson's land, weft bow
Simpson Alexander, merc. taylor, foot of pleasance
Simpson John, taylor, Ahson's square
Simpsons Mifs, tobbacconifts, oppofite the exchange
Simpson Walter, grocer. potter-row
Simpson, vintner, oppofite the tolbooth door
Simpson Mifs, weft bow
Simpson John, new tap-room, oppofite regifter office
Simpson John, merchant, head of pleasance
Simpson Walter, clerk, brifto ftreet
Sinclair Lady, Crichton's ftreet
Sinclair Robert, Efq. advocate, Prince's ftreet
Sinclair William, brewer, St Leonard's
Sinclair Mrs, fountain clofe
Sinclair Mrs, chaple ftreet
Sinclair John, merchant, caftle-hill
Sinclair Lady, Argyles fquare
Sinclar Alex. of Barrock, Gairdner's land, canongate
Sinclair Mifs, merchant, luckenbooths
Sinclair John, of Friezwick, Efq. fociety
Sinclair Geo. writer to the fig. Pirrie's clofe, canon.
Sinclair Andrew, writer, James' court
Sinclair Robert, advocate, Miln's fquare
Sinclair Mrs, Foulis' clofe
Sinclair John, feedfman, weft bow foot
Sinclair Alexander, taylor, potter-row
Sivewright William, potter-row port
Sivewright James, comb-maker, foot of blackfriars wy
Sivewright Mrs, Herriot's work bridge
Skae David, grocer, oppofite the guard
Skae Robert, tobacconift, head of Peeble's wynd
Skene General, abbey-hill
Skene John, meffenger, at A. Fifhers, vintner, crofs
Skeill David, merchant, meal market
Skinner James, writer, Kincaid's land, cowgate
Skinner Andrew, land furveyor, Kincaid's land, cow.
Skirving William, writer, Nicolfon's ftreet
Skirving John, watch maker, parliament fquare
Skelton Thomas, flater, flefh-market clofe, canongate

Slorach Robert, taylor, portſburgh
Slorach John, taylor, briſto-ſtreet
Smart Robert, ſmith, calton
Small Charles, vintner, Craig's cloſe
Small Mrs, confectioner, canongate head
Small Charles, hair-dreſſer, back of the guard
Small George, cooper, oppoſite Cheſſel's court
Small James, ſhoe-maker, Aliſon's ſquare
Smeall John, glazier, Libberton's wynd
Smellie William, printer, anchor cloſe
Smith Donald, & Co merchts. W. wing of the exch.
Smith Robert, writer, Turk's cloſe
Smith George, currier, weſt port
Smith Robert, taylor, head of Leith wynd
Smith Mrs, of Methven, St Andrew's ſquare
Smith David, advocate, St Andrew's ſquare
Smith Robert, grocer, head of Foulis' cloſe
Smith John, writer to the ſignet, briſto ſtreet
Smith James, writer to the ſignet Geddes' cloſe
Smith John, writer, Geddes' cloſe
Smith William, writer, caſtle hill
Smith James, writer, caſtle hill
Smith Adam, ſkinner, ſtock bridge
Smith Gilbert, founder, St Ninian's row
Smith James, founder, canal ſtreet
Smith William, merchant, luckenbooths
Smith Mrs, baxter, back of the guard
Smith David, baxter, oppoſite Aliſon's ſquare
Smith William, baker, potter-row well
Smith John, wright, St Ninian's row
Smith William, maſon, croſs cauſey
Smith Miſs, mantua maker, Peebie's wynd
Smith Peter, taylor, canongate head
Smith James, ſtay maker, canongate head
Smith James, ſlater, foot of the canongate
Smith James, ſhoemaker, oppoſite new ſtreet
Smith Robert, ſhoemaker, chapel ſtreet
Smith John, ſhoemaker, gooſe dub
Smith James, limner, end of prince's ſtreet
Smith Nathaniel, leather dealer, Aliſon's ſquare
Smith Peter, keeper of mortality rec Forreſter's w.
Smith David, tea and ſpirit dealer, front of exchange

Smith James, glover, creams
Smith Mrs, confectioner, cowgate head
Smith   , writer, horse wynd
Smith John, stabler, head of the pleasance
Smart Robert, smith, calton
Smith Miss, mantua-maker, Forrester's wynd
Smith Mrs, Nicolson's street
Smith David, grocer, abbey strand
Smith Mrs, grocer, opposite Milton's lodging can.
Smith James, writer, head of lady Stair's close
Smith Mrs, castle hill
Smith Thomas, merchant, bow head well
Smith Wil. clerk to A. Crichton, op. Queensb. lodg.
Smith Andrew, hair dresser, below bridge street
Smith Thomas, writer, Argyle's square
Smith William, stabler, foot of the pleasance
Smiton Charles, hatter, head of blackfriars wynd
Smiton Alexander, book binder, Brown's close
Smiton John, musician, head of blackfriars wynd
Smiton Walter, coach painter, Brown's close
Smollet Mrs, Crichton street
Smollet Mrs, St John's street
Somervell Samuel, baxter, west bow head
Somervell David, tobacconist, grass market, south side
Somervell Patrick, lint-dresser, op. the exchange
Somervell James, cooper, twopenny custom
Somervell James, stabler, grass market
Somervell John, wheel wright, grass market
Somervell Mrs, Somervill's land canongate
Sommers James, writer, covenant close
Sommers Thomas, king's glazier, flesh market close
Sommers Thomas, vintner, op. the guard
Sommers Thomas, vintner, Dunbar's close
Sommers Mrs, merchant, head of Libberton's wynd
Spalding James, grocer, op. the tron church
Spalding Charles, confecti. mint close and exchange
Spalding John, saddler, grass market
Spalding Mrs, bunkers hill
Spalding Gordon Alexander, bunkers hill
Spalding Charles, bookseller, canongate head
Spankie Miss, milliner, anchor close
Spankie James, stay maker, canongate head

Spark Peter, writer, Charles' street

Spark Tho. perf and clothes cleaner, Robertson's cl.

Spence James, writer, old bank close

Spens Nathaniel, physician, Niddery's wynd

Spence David, physician, Wardrope's court——His lving in hospital, Campbell's close, cowgate

Spence Ja. t' cal. to the bank of Scotland, bank close

Spence Laurence, writer, Gosford's close

Spence William, lawn market, N side

Spence David, linen manufact. fountain bridge

Spence Thomas, weaver, canon mills

Spence Mrs, taylor, lawn market

Spence John, painter, below the pipe close

Spence James, hair-dresser, clam shell turnpike

Spence Robert, dentist, Miln's court

Spotiswood James, of Dunipace. Esq, cross causey

Spotiswood John, of that ilk, meal market stairs

Spotiswood James, paper maker, h. of Niddry's wy.

Spotiswood Wil. iron monger, grass market, S. side

Spotiswood J. feedm & iron monger, west bow foot

Sprott William, procurator, Morocco's close, canong.

Sprott Walter, wright, calton

Sprott James, tanner, portsburgh

Sprott Alexander, tanner, cross causey

Sprott John, candle-maker, h. of blackfriars wynd

Sprott Robert, candle-maker, at the tron church

Squair John, flesher, flesh market close

Staig John, wright, opposite foot of Peebles wynd

Stark John, wright, bristo street

Stark George, comb-maker, shoe makers close canon.

Stark John, tobacconist, opposite the exchange

Stark George, comb maker, W. end of luckenbooth

St Clair Andrew, banker, Nicolson's street

St Clair Charles, advocate, St John's street

St Clair Mrs, Argyle's square

Stalker James, teacher of English, Paterson's court

Steedman John, physician, St John's street

Steedman Robert, room-setter, potter row

Steedman James, musical instru. maker, west bow h.

Steedman Charles, wright, below Queensberry lodg.

Steedman William, tool maker, potter-row

Steadman and Smith, milliners, head of fountain close
Steadman Mrs, room-fetter, Henderson's stairs
Steele Robert, confectioner, opposite bridge street
Steele Alexander, wright, goose dub
Steele John, wheel-wright, foot of blackfriars wynd
Steele George, smith, Gabriel's road
Steele David, merchant, foot of meal market stairs
Steele Andrew, writer, patterson's court
Stenhouse Mrs, princes street
Stenhouse Thomas, smith, canongate foot
Steven George, accomptant, baxters close lawn mark.
Steven John, writer, castle-hill
Steven Alexander, brewer, water of Leith
Steven Patrick, merchant, bishops land close
Steven Mrs, baxter, head of Blackfriars wynd
Steven James, lint-dresser, foot of the cross causey
Steven Christopher, barber, below Queensberry lodg.
Sephens K. and A. uppermost baxters close
Stephens Mrs, cowgate head
Stephens James, shoe-maker, Charles' street
Stephens David, trunk-maker, lawn market N. side
Stephenson Robert, painter, Shakespeare square
Stevenson John, merchant, head of luckenbooths
Stevenson Alexander, advocate, h. of Borthwick's cl.
Stevenson Doctor, bow foot
Stevenson Alex dep. clerk of session, Niddery's wy.
Stevenson Mrs, George's square
Stevenson William, stabler, grass-market
Stevenson Mrs, St Agnes street
Stevenson John, pump-maker, portsburgh
Stevenson Alexander, smith, abbey-hill
Stewart Patrick, grocer, head of the flesh market cl.
Stewart Charles, writer, covenant close
Stewart Archibald of Stewarthall, op chapel of ease
Stewart John, writer, bristo street
Stewart Adam, writer, Leith wynd
Stewart Robert, leather merchant, Nicolson's street
Stewart Miss, of Binny, Cant's close
Stewart Mrs, of Barnhill's, canongate
Stewart Sir John, of Allenbank, advoc. St John's st.
Stewart William, advocate, Milu's square
Stewart Daniel, macer of exchequer, Baron Maul's cl.

Stuart Andrew, jun. writer to the fignet, fociety
Stuart Mathew, profeffor, college
Stuart David, writer to the fignet, Elphinfton's court
Stuart John, extractor covenant clofe
Stuart Thomas, fecr. to the old bank, Miln's fquare
Stewart Archibald, merchant, fcinnes
Stewart James, writer to the fignet, Adam's fquare
Stewart James, extractor, Cleland's yards
Stewart William, junr. writer, broughton
Stewart Charles, writer, brifto ftreet
Stewart Robert, writer, old bank clofe
Stewart James, writer, Turk's clofe
Stewart George, profeffor, college
Stewart Robert, glazier, canongate head
Stewart John, clock and watch maker, mint clofe
Stewart James, druggift, bull turnpike
Stewart Neil, mufic fhop, parliament fquare
Stewart William, grocer, head of lady Stair's clofe
Stewart Mrs, grocer, foot of Burnet's clofe
Stewart Alexander, grocer, Nicolfon's ftreet
Stewart Daniel, grocer, op. foot of Forrefter's wynd
Stewart Malcolm, taylor, Nicolfon's ftreet
Stewart Alexander, taylor, blackfriars wynd,
Stewart Alexander, fhoemaker, Peeble's wynd
Stewart Robert, wright, Nicolfon's ftreet
Stewart James, wright, portfburgh
Stewart David, glover, at the tolbooth church door
Stewart John, vintner, head of writer's court
Stewart James, horfe hyrer, grafs market
Stewart Patrick, rope maker, grafs market
Stewart Mrs, room fetter, Gavinloch's land
Stewart Mrs, room fetter, Turk's clofe
Stewart Duncan, printer, Currie's clofe
Stewart Alexander, hair dreffer, bridge ftreet
Stewart David, poft-office ftairs, third door
Stewart William, writer, Turk's clofe
Stewart Mifs, weft port
Stewart Mrs, Nicolfon's ftreet
Stewart of Eaft Craigs Alifon's fquare
Stewart Major, back of the canongate

N

Stewart the Honourable David, St Andrew's square
Stewart   , bridge-street
Stewart Selkirk, captain, bunkers hill
Stewart William, and Co. bridge street
Stewart Mrs, Tweedale's clofe
Stewart Mrs, Foulis clofe
Stewart George, grocer, cowgate head
Stewart George, printer, briflo-ftreet
Stewart John, fherriff fubftitute, baillie Grants clofe
Stewart Robert, meal-monger, grafs-market
Stewart Mrs, Adam's fquare
Still Robert, writer, netherbow
Stirling James, banker, luckenbooths
Stirling Mrs, Brown's clofe
Stirling John, hofier, netherbow
Stirling Andrew, fifhmonger, Peeble's wynd
Stobie John, writer, Warrifton's clofe
Stodart James, Efq, Strachan's clofe
Stoddart and Fairbairn, wine merch. chapel ftreet
Stoddart James, fhoemaker, broughton
Stoddart Mrs, advocate's clofe
Stories Miffes, haberdafhers, luckenbooths
Storie Alex. candle maker, h. of Borthwick's clofe
Storie John, grocer, grafs market
Storie Mrs, baxter, luckenbooths
Storrie William, writer, St Mary's wynd
Storie John, grocer, St David's ftreet
Storrie John, pen-maker, Leith wynd
Stormonth James, writer, cowgate head
Strachan Mrs, Heriot's work bridge
Strachan Mrs, caftle hill
Strachan Francis, writer to the fignet, Warrifton's cl.
Strachan William, grocer, briflo ftreet
Strachan Mifs, keeps lady boarders, lochend's clofe
Strachan John, fmith, crofs caufey
Strachan William, fhoemaker, crofs caufey
Straiton William, chaife hyrer, foot of the pleafance
Straiton William, fmith, pleafence
Straiton John, brewer, two penny cuftom,
Straiton Archibald, watch maker, Don's clofe
Strange David, dancing mafter, Todderick's wynd
Sturrock J. tea and fpirit dealer, h. of Leith wynd

Sutherland countefs of, George's fquare
Sutherland Wil. fifh hook maker, Leith wynd
Sutherland Alex. glover, Hay's l. grafs market
Sutherland Mrs, midwife, Peeble's wynd
Sutherland Mrs, room fetter, Borthwick's clofe
Sutherland James, at C. Elliot's parliament fquare
Sutherland John, writer, oppofite the chapel of eafe
Sutherland Mrs, midwife, foot of Campbell's clofe
Sutherland John, lint-dreffer, oppofite new ftreet
Suttar James, ftay-maker netherbow
Suttie Sir George, Argyle's fquare
Suttie Mrs, new ftreet
Swan George, jeweller, head of Carrubber's clofe
Swan James, hair dreffer, meal market ftairs
Swanfton William, writing mafter, new bank clofe
Swanfton J. clerk, poft office, flefh market cl. canong.
Swanfton John, grocer, below Carrubber's clofe
Swinton John, fenr. advocate, Crichton ftreet
Swinton John, jun. Brown's fquare
Swinton Mrs, Teviot row
Swinton Mifs, fociety
Swinton Mrs, Charles' ftreet
Swinton William, wright, abbey hill
Sword Mrs, cowgate head
Sydferf William, teacher, Hyndford's clofe
Symmer Mrs, thiftle court
Symmington Jofeph, brewer, abbey clofe
Symmington Mrs, baker, grafs market
Symington George, brewer, abbey

T

Tailour Alexander, Efq; calton hill
Tailour Mrs, Borthwick's clofe
Tailour David, attorn. in excheq. new affembly clofe
Tailour Ja. wr. to the fig. Kennedy's clofe, caftle hill
Tailour Alexander, furgeon, crofs caufey
Tailour William, brewer, abbey hill
Tailour Alexr. goldfmith, Rattray's clofe, cowgate
Tailour William, merchant, luckenbooths
Tailour Robert, founder, St Ninian's row
Taylor John, merchant, luckenbooths
Taylor William, accomptant in the excife, brifto ftr.
Tailor John, gold-fmith, parliament fquare

Taylor Mrs, abbey strand

Taylor Peter, student, at Mr Wymfs, silk dyer, cow.

Taylor John, writer to the fignet, old assembly close

Tailour Robert, baxter, above the canongate church

Tailour David grocer, cowgate foot

Tailour John, baker, potter-row

Tailour John, grocer, west port

Tailour Patrick, Scot's close cowgate

Tailour Mrs, room-fetter, op meal market stairs

Tailour Robert, baker, below the canongate church

Tailour Mrs, grocer, oppofite meal market stairs

Tailor Thomas, officer of excife, S. back of canon.

Tait John, writer to the fignet, Shakefpeare fquare

Tait Alex principal clerk of feffion, Argyle's fquare

Tait james, writer, foot of Lady Stair's close

Tait James, fenior, wright, foot of Stonelaws close

Tait James, junior, brufh maker, head of cowgate

Tait Robert, fhoe-maker, head of the pleafance

Tait Walter, merchant, two penny custom

Tawfe John, writer, Flemings close cowgate

Telfair Mrs, of Scotftown, St John's ftreet

Tennants Mifs, bailie Fyfe's close

Tenant Francis, flefher, flefh market close

Tenant Mrs, mid-wife, Blackfriars wynd

Tenant George, heel maker, Merlin's wynd

Tenies Mifs, Princes ftreet

Thain Mrs, merchant, lawn market

Thom Mrs, Gabriel's road

Thom Willam, deacon of the weavers head of Nid. w.

Thomas Mifs, tea, china, glafs and ftone ware dealer
   front of Cheffels' court

Thomas Mifs, fountain close

Thomfon Mifs, Barrengers close

Thomfon Mrs, Boyd's close

Thomfon Mifs, back row

Thomfon Alex. of cuftoms, back of weigh houfe

Thomfon Alex writer to fignet, Halkerfton's wynd

Thomfon John, writer to fignet, St Andrew's ftreet

Thomfon Thomas, teller in the bank, Gabriel's road

Thomfon Mrs, above Balfour's coffee-houfe

Thomfon Alexander, clerk to excife, potter-row

Thomfon Walter, kings macer, Sellars' close

Thomson jun. merchant, grafs market, N. fide
Thomson John, merchant, fountain bridge
Thomson James, mafon, foot of new ftreet
Thomson John, mathematician, Skinners clofe]
Thomson James, glover, creams, or Morrocco's clofe
Thomson John, taylor, Gabriel's road
Thomson Alexander, grocer, head of Borthwick's cl.
Thomson William, taylor, cowgate head
Thomson John, carver and gilder, Magdalen's chapel
Thomson James, baxter, head of Forrefter's wynd
Thomson James, writing-mafter, Niddery's wynd
Thomson James, junior, merchant, Carrubber's clofe
Thomson Charles, merchant, calton
Thomson Robert, merchant, exchange
Thomson James, founder, weft bow
Thomson John, barber, foot of Cant's clofe
Thomson James, wright, weft bow
Thomson Alexander, grocer, portfburgh
Rhomson James, ferrier, broughton
Thomson David, tool-maker, mint clofe
Thomson John, fpatterdafh maker, op. Cheffel's c.
Thomson George, plafterer, portfburgh
Thomson William, barber, weft bow
Thomson John, mufician, lauriefton
Thomson Andrew, tobacconift, h. of bridge ftreet
Thomson James, writer, Dickfon's clofe
Thomson John, merchant, writers court
Thomson Robert, meffenger, Gavinloch's l. lawn m.
Thomson William, druggift, head of Niddery's wynd
Thomson James, taylor, Nicolfon's ftreet
Thomson John, flefher, flefh market clofe
Thomson Alexander, writer, uppermoft baxters cl.
Thomson Mrs, Hyndford's clofe
Thomson and Blyth, joiners, hard well clofe, pleaf.
Thomson Maurice, brewer, portfburgh
Thomson Patrick, at Giles wright, college wynd
Thomson Mrs, bow foot
Thomson Mifs fchool-miftrefs, covenant clofe
Thomson Mifs Libberton's wynd
Thomson John, wright, college wynd
Thomson William, grocer, cowgate head
Thomson John, retail. of liquors, f. of Campbell's cl.

Thomſon Mrs, oppoſite linen hall

Thomſon David, taylor, fleſh market cloſe canongate

Thomſon Mrs, St Andrew's ſtreet

Thomſon Mrs, canongate

Thomſon Mrs, ſchool miſtreſs, Jackſon's cloſe

Thoburn Thomas, ſurgeon, M'Farlane's l portſburgh

Threipland Sir Stewart, phyſician, Biſhop's land

Thriepland Mis, Biſhop's land

Tibbets Thomas, hatter, head of new bank cloſe

Tindal William, glaſs grinder, Bell's wynd

Tod Mrs, wind miln ſtreet

Tod Mrs, St John's ſtreet

Tod Rhomas, writer to ſignet, George's ſquare

Tod and Talloway, merchants, luckenbooths

Tod John. merchant, Crichton ſtreet

Tod Thomas, merchants, Blyth's cloſe

Tod Henry, cabinet-maker, upholſterer and undertaker, new ſtreet canongate

Tod Mrs, caſtle hill

Tod Mrs, oppoſite new ſtreet canongate

Tod George, writer, blackfriars wynd

Tod George, writer, Riddle's land

Torphichen Lady, ſociety

Torry James, merchant, front of Exchange.—Houſe
Gabriel's road

Touch John, miniſter, Crichton's entry

Touch Walter, ſtay-maker, St Mary's wynd

Touch George, bell hanger, old aſſembly cloſe

Touch Thomas, baſket maker, foot of Peebles wynd

Toutar James, ſtay-maker, mint

Townſend, baſket-maker, op, foot of Forreſter's wy.

Trail James, ſtationer, parliament ſquare

Traquair, Ladies of, canongate head

Traquair John, ſtone ware merchant, Charles' ſtreet

Trelawney Lady, Argyles ſquare

Trotter Thomas, of Mortonhall, Eſq; Taylor's l. can.

Trotter Archibald, of Buſh, Herriot's cloſe

Trotter John, merchant, fleſh market cloſe

Trotter Mis, Gentle's cloſe, canongate

Trotter and Co. confect. and grocers, weſt bow head

Trotter Robert, writer to ſig. Herriot's cloſe canong.

Trotter Thomas, upholſterer, Miln's court

Tullias James, wright, Middleton's entry
Tulloch Thomas, wine merchant, lawn mark. N•side
Turnbull Mrs, of Currie, Crichton street
Turnbull John, brewer, canal street
Turnbull Mrs, of Stonehill, chapel street
Turnbull Mrs, Libberton's wynd
Turnbull Mrs, grafs market, fouth fide
Turnbull & Aitchifon, watch makers, back of guard
Turnbull George, jun. baxter, brifto street
Turnbull Thomas, merchant, front of exchange
Turnbull George, fen baxter, potter-row
Turnbull John, taylor, foot of the pleafance
Tnrhbull Robert, flater, college wynd
Turner David, cooper, cowgate-head
Tweedie Alexander, printer, Dunbar's clofe
Tyrie John, writer, Kinloch's clofe
Tytler Alexander, advocate, Shakefpeare fquare
Tytler William, writer to fignet, Campbell's clofe

U

Udney Alex commiffioner of excife, George's fquare
Urquhart Leonard, writer to fignet, Forrefter's wynd
Urquhart William, writer to fignet, Forrefter's wynd
Urquhart and Richardfon, taylors, canongate head
Urquhart Mrs, room-fetter, Dickfon's clofe
Urquhart John, writer, Forrefter's wynd

V

Vair Will. wig-maker, head of the old affembly clofe
Vair   , writer, baillie Fyfe's clofe
Vair Mifs, Mrs, teviot row
Veevers William, druggift, lawn-market
Veitch Mifs, grocer, goofe dub
Veitch Mifs, mantua-maker, potter-row
Veitch William, mafon, St Andrew's fquare
Veitch John, marble-cutter, canongate foot
Veitch George, grocer, wind-mill ftreet
Veitch George, jun wine merchant, Nicolfon's ftreet.
Vernon Mrs Leith wynd
Vint Thomas, writer, St Mary's wynd
Voggery Mrs, Libberton's wynd
Vyes Mrs, Charles ftreet
Vyes John, Charles ftreet

W

Waddel Mifs, of Craw-hill, Murdoch's clofe
Waddel Mifs, mantua-maker, exchange
Waddel Thomas, taylor, cowgate head
Waddel Henry, wr. at Mr Reid's wright. college wy.
Wait William, Efq. Hanover-ftreet
Walker John, and Co. Chalmers' clofe
Walker James, auctioneer, foot of Libberton's wynd
Walker Mrs, brifto-ftreet
Walker David, advocate, Dickfon's clofe
Walker William, writer, blackfriars wynd
Walker James, writer to the fignet, fociety
Walker Robert, minifter, caftle-hill
Walker James, fpirit dealer oppo. Stonelaw's cl. cow.
Walker William, writer, and attorney in the exche-
    quer, Byres' clofe
Walker Robert, furgeon, Sellar' clofe
Walker Mrs, brewer, old play houfe clofe
Walker Robert, tanner, old play houfe clofe
Walker James, engraver, calton
Walker Mrs, ftabler, grafs market, fouth fide
Walker James, grocer, back of the guard
Walker William, grocer, fountain bridge
Walker Alex. fchoolmafter, Robertfon's clofe, cowg.
Walker Charles, vintner, writer's court
Walker Alexander, room fetter, writer's court
Walker Mrs, midwife, Campbell's clofe, canongate
Walker Alexander, hofier, head of Gosford's clofe
Walker John, ftabler, grafs market
Walker James, Efq: caftle hill
Walker James, merchant, luckenbooths
Walker John, merchant, baron Grant's clofe
Walker Mrs, ftabler, grafs market
Walker Andrew, malt mill maker, crofs caufey
Walker Mrs, Kinloch's clofe
Walkinfhaw Mrs, St John's ftreet
Walkinfhaw Mrs, Niddery's wynd
Wallace Mrs, of Cairn-hill, fouth Gray's clofe
Wallace lady, Hanover ftreet
Wallace Alexander, banker, James's court
Wallace and Fullerton Miffes, Gosford's clofe
Wallace William, advocate, head of Brodie s clofe

Wallace Charles, hofier, front of the exchange
Wallace William, ftabler, grafs market
Wallace Richard, baxter, fountainbridge
Wallace Robert, Alifon's fquare
Wallace David, writer, calton hill
Wallace Lady, St Andrew's ftreet
Wallace Mifs, Libberton's wynd
Ward William, inn keeper, now at Muffelburgh
Ward Mrs, Nicolfon's ftreet
Warden John, minifter, Tod's land, canongate
Warden George, ftabler, grafs market
Wardrobe Andrew, furgeon, Strichen's clofe
Wardrobe David, broughton
Wardrobe David, furgeon, Forrefter's wynd
Wardrope Ralph, grocer, foot of caftle wynd
Wares Francis, vintner, anchor clofe
Warrender Hugh, writer, caftle hill
Warrender George, Efq, Brunt field links
Warrenders Miffes, George's ftreet
Waterfton Wil. wax chandler, f of Dunba-'s clofe
Watterfton Robert, barber, f. of Warrifton's clofe
Watterfton Robert, ftay-maker, mint clofe
Watfon Mrs, of Pilmor, Libberton's wynd
Watfon Mis, Heriot's work bridge
Watfon Thomas, glazier, foot of Toderick's wynd
Watfon Mrs, St Mary's wynd
Watfon Mrs, Carrubber's clofe
Watfon James, writer to the fignet, Miln's court
Watfon Alexander, writer, Craig's clofe
Watfon John, procurator, Miln's court
Watfon Samuel, procurator, meal market ftairs
Watfon James, painter, Hyndford's clofe
Watfon Robert, hard ware merchant, luckenbooths
Watfon John, merchant, Leith wynd
Watfon William, & Co. wrights, Weir's cl canong.
Watfon Alexander, grocer, newington
Watfon Thomas, taylor, foot of Toderick's wynd
Watfon Thomas, fmith, pleafance
Watfon George, wool merchant, weft bow head
Watfon Samuel, tobacconift, oppofite the guard
Watfon George, fhoemaker, Nicolfon's ftreet

Watson John, schoolmaster, upper common close, can.

Watson Andrew, plaisterer, Leith wynd

Watson James, barber, Gabriel's road

Watson James, messenger, anchor close

Watson Alexander, excise officer, castle hill

Watson James, junr. messenger, Don's close

Watson John, potter, west pans, nigh Musselburgh, sells all kinds of Brown ware

Watson David, linen-manufactorer, old assembly close

Watt John, writer, Forrester's wynd

Watt George, founder, St Ninian's row

Watt John, grocer, bristo street

Watt Alexander, wright, Toderick's wynd

Watt John, shoemaker, opposite meal-market

Watt Mark, tobacconist, west bow foot

Wauchope John, writer to the signet, horse wynd

Waugh James, baker, water of Leith

Waugh Miss, potter-row

Waugh John, basket maker, flesh market close

Webster Alexander, minister, castle hill

Webster David, baxter, St Ninian's row

Webster, Charles, physician, St Andrew's street

Weir Alexander, Middleton's entry

Weir Alexander, painter, Toderick's wynd

Weir James, wright, calton

Weir John, shoe-maker, Gray's close

Weir James, wright, at Tollcross

Wellwood Robert, of Garvock, Esq; St Andrew's sq.

Welsh John, writer, to the signet, fountain close

Welsh James, jeweller, parliament square

Welsh John, goldsmith, under the tolboooth

Welsh Harry, writer, new street

Welsh Miss, milliner, front of the exchange

Wemyss the hon. James, of Wemyss, St John street

Wemyss Sir James, Riddle's close

Wemyss lieutenant governor, in the castle

Wemyss Mrs, op Queensberry's lodging

Wemyss William, writer to the signet, Merlin's wynd

Wemyss James, jeweller, near council chamber door

Wemyss John, silk dyer, f. of Dick's close, cowg.

Wemyss Robert, school master, plainstone close, can.

Wemyss Robert, silk dyer, head of west bow

West James, shoemaker, fountain well
Westwater James, coachmaker, cowgate port
Westwater Patrick, whip maker, horse wynd
Wharton Thomas, commiss. of excise, lauriston
White James, candle maker, Kincaid's land, cowgate
White Alexander, merchant, Chalmers' close
White Bain, writer, west bow head
White John captain, high school yards
White John, grocer, canongate head
White George, tanner, head of the pleasance
White James, barber, foot of Libberton's wynd
White John, merchant, west bow
White James, taylor, cross cauley
White John, taylor, abbey hill
White George, stay-maker, cowgate port
White William, baxter, grange gateside
White & Mitchell, toymen & jewellers, op. tron ch.
White David, merchant, foot of Niddrey's wynd
White Peter, grocer, Paterson's court
White George, baxter, calton
White Robert, smith, portsburgh
White James, jun. hair dresser, lawn market
White Mrs, of Milton, op. Milton's lodging
White William, iron monger, opposite the guard
White James, merchant, Chalmers' close
White James, Kincaid's land
Whitebanks lady, potter-row
Whitefoord Sir John, advocate, St Andrew's square
Whitehead Robert, wright, Jack's close
Whitehead John, grocer, Nicolson's street
Whitney Mrs, Seller's close
Wight Alexander, advocate, St Andrew's street
Wight George, surgeon, opposite the linen hall
Wight David, writer, St Andrew's square
Wight Robert, merchant, head of luckenbooths
Wight David, baxter, cowgate foot
Wight William, turner, Niddrey's wynd
Wight Robert, baxter, opposite the exchange
Wight William, baxter, nether bow
Wight Mrs, St Andrew's square
Wight Miss, merchant, lawn market
Wight Alexander, writer, Turk's close

Wight Mrs, hoop-maker, foot of horfe wynd
Wight Mrs, Nicolfon's ftreet
Wightman William, baker, Nicolfon's ftreet
Wightman Edward, wright, pleafance
Wild John, tobbacconift, below the flefh market clofe
Wilkie Mrs, George's fquare
Wilkie Robert, candle maker, grafs market
Wilkie David, brifto ftreet
Wilkie William, taylor, canal ftreet
Wilkie Mrs. old affembly clofe
Wilkiefon Mrs, fountain clofe
Williams   , ladies hair dreffer, luckenbooths
Williams Mrs, room fetter, old cuftom houfe ftairs
Williamfon Jofeph, advocate, Leven lodge
Williamfon Jofeph, jun. Leven lodge
Williamfon David, writer, leven lodge
Williamfon Andrew, nail maker, Leith wynd
Williamfon Alexander, factor to lord Hope, Nicol. ftr.
Williamfon Bruce, furgeon, Nicolfon's ftreet
Williamfon Mifs, of Carkdronie, h. of high fchol wy.
Williamfon Andrew, merchant, weft bow
Williamfon Alexander, Nicolfon's ftreet
Williamfon James, flefher, flefh market clofe
Williamfon Thomas, flefher, flefh market clofe
Williamfon William, mercer, Nicolfon's ftreet
Williamfon Charles, fchool-mafter, new ftreet
Williamfon Mrs, room fetter, head of Leith wynd
Williamfon Mrs, room-fetter, new ftreet
Williamfon Geo. meffenger, undermoft meal-mark ft.
Williamfon James, hair-dreffer, head of the cowgate
Willifon David, printer, Craig's clofe
Willifon George, fhoe-maker, calton
Willfon John, bookfeller, prefidents ftairs
Willfon James, fmith, Hume's clofe
Willfon Robert, writer, britifh coffee houfe
Willfon Adam and Co. hard ware-merchants, lucken.
Willfon Mrs, Winton's land canongate
Willfon John, merchant, lawn market
Willfon Mrs, room-fetter, makes graves cloaths in the
    neateft manner, foot of the Prefident's ftairs
Willfon Thomas, taylor, fountain clofe
Willfon Mrs, Niddery's wynd

Wilson William, writer, old excise office cowgate
Wilson Mrs, Nicolson's street
Wilson Alexander, bristo street
Wilson Miss, Paterson's court
Wilson Robert, junr Borthwick's close
Wilson Alexander, merchant, castle hill
Wilson William, junr. writer, old excise office
Wilson Mrs grocer, Shakespear's square
Wilson William, writer to the signet, new bank close
Wilson John, mason, Shakespeare square
Wilson Archibald, painter, St Mary's wynd
Wilsons Robert, sen. & Richard, printers, Hume's cl.
Wilson Robert, jun and Co. printers, foot of the new
    bank close.—House, Borthwick's close
Wilson Ebenezer, founder, Libberton's wynd
Wilson Thomas, linen manufacturer, canongate foot
Wilson Andrew, merchant, head of the old bank close
Wilson Peter, silk dyer, op Nicolson's street potter-r,
Wilson Andrew, baxter, Nicolson's street
Wilson Andrew, flesher, flesh market close
Wilson James, smith, Leith wynd
Wilson Thomas, keeper of the linen hall, canongate
Wilson Mrs, midwife opposite meal market
Wilson Thomas, writer, castle hill
Wilson John, heckle-maker, cross-causey
Wilson Mrs, grocer, canongate foot
Wilsons Misses, mantua makers, Geddes' close
Wilson Robert, wheel wright, oppo. head of new st.
Wilson John, silver turner, Libberton's wynd
Wilson Thomas, grocer, cowgate port
Winter James, coach maker, back of canongate
Winter George, hair dresser, head of Chalmers' close
Winter William, shoe-maker, calton
Winter William, barber, old assembly close
Wiseman Alexander, wright, flesh market close
Wishart George, minister, shoe makers close canong.
Wishart John, slater, candle maker-row
Wishaw Lady, St John's street
Wood Mrs, Nicolson's street
Wood George, of Warriston, pleasance
Wood David, vintner, Morrocco's close
Wood John, captain, Charles' street

Wood William, captain, middle of the canongate
Wood Alexander, furgeon, exchange
Wood Andrew, furgeon, Morrison's clofe
Wood Jafper, furgeon, chapel ftreet
Wood John, bookfeller, luckenbooths
Wood John, tackfman Herriot's gardens
Wood James, taylor, canongate head
Wood Mrs, grocer, oppofite foot of back ftairs
Wood John, officer of excife, candle maker-row
Wood Lady, Murdoch's clofe
Wood Thomas, furgeon, new bank clofe
Woodhead Anthony, procurator, Forrefter's wynd
Wordie John, barker, James' court
Wotherfpoon Thomas, wheel-wright, grafs market
Wright Daniel, joiner Drummond's land canongate
Wright Robert, above Balfour's coffee houfe
Wright John, teacher of mathematics, Kennedy's clofe
Wright Charles, ftationer, parliament fquare
Wright John, writer, brifto ftreet
Wright John, baxter, nether bow
Wright William, joiner, Leith wynd
Wright Malcolm merchant, lawn market
Wright James, pewterer, brifto ftreet
Wright Mrs, keeps boarders, Nicolfon's ftreet
Wright John, baxter, head of fountain clofe
Wright David, oilfeller high fchool yards
Wright Thomas, Efq; Turtle court
Wright Mifs, milliner, Miln's court
Wyvil E general furvey. of excife, Panmuir's cl. can.

Y

Yair Mrs, bookfeller, parliament fquare
Yairs Miffes, milliners, luckenbooths
Yeaman John, mathemat. inftrum. maker, bow head
Yellowlees John, grocer, h. of lochend's clofe, can.
Yetts Mifs, keeps boarders, Dickfon's clofe
Yetts William, hair-dreffer, front of Miln's court
Young Robert, upholfterer, Paterfon's court
Young Mrs, Sellars' clofe
Young John, haberdafher, op new bridge
Young Mitchell, painter, Morifon's clofe
Young William, baxter, head of fkinner's clofe
Young Alexander, writing mafter, blackfriars wynd

Young William, joiner, Leith wynd

Young William, school master, bristo street

Young James, writer, Foulis close

Young   , covenant close

Young John, writer, Warriston's close

Young Mrs, below St John's street

Young Mrs, Leith wynd

Young Mrs, blackfriars wynd

Young Mrs, Chalmers' close

Young Thomas, physician, new street

Young William, writer, writer's court

Young John, writer, Foulis' close

Young Mrs, lady Stair's close

Young William, joiner, Leith wynd

Young Alexander, writer, bristo street

Young Edward, procurator, Rainy's land, west bow

Young John, wright, thistle court

Young Alexr. wright, Shakespeare square

Young William, wright, flesh market close, canong.

Young William, Scot's close, cowgate

Young Thomas, schoolmaster, president stairs

Young John, writing master, Dickson's close

Young and Trotter, upholsterers, luckenbooths——Cabinet ware room, prince's street

Young John, merchant, grass market

Young Mrs, stabler, cowgate head

Young John, taylor, Boyd's close

Young John, smith, entry to Nicolson's street

Young John, shoemaker, Richmond street

Young Ja. wig maker & hair dresser, bull turnpike

Young Robert, stabler, cross causey

Young and Jollie, cork cutters, west port

Younger Archibald Campbell, brewer, abbey

Yule Benjamin, baxter, front of Miln's court

Yule Andrew, tobacconist, op. the tolbooth

Z

Ziegler George, writer, cowgate head

Ziegler Alexander, goldsmith, Alison's square

LEITH DIRECTORY.

AIR Duncan, ship-master, on the shore
Alexander Mrs ship-master, Bernard-street
Alexander Robert, watch-maker, tolbooth wynd
Aliton Alex. dep. cashier of excise, head of the links
Aliton Alexander, sail and rope-maker on the links
Allan David, officer of excise, opposite the pipes
Anderson John, merchant, kirkgate
Anderson Andrew, treasurer to the trinity-house, longatefide
Anderson Alexander, brewer, yard-heads
Anderson George, kirkgate
Anderson Mrs cork-cutter, rotten-row
Anderson James and Co. merchants, tolbooth wynd
Archibald John, wine-merchant, kirkgate
Armstrong James, wig-maker, tolbooth wynd

B
Baird George, brewer, dub-row
Band and Orrock, grocers, sheriff-brae
Band Andrew, foot of Leith walk
Balfour Ja. adv. justice of peace, at Pilrig, near Leith
Balfour Henry, wine-merchant, king's street
Ballom James, wright, Lee's quarter
Ballantyne Mrs milliner, opposite the pipes
Buker Thomas, brewer, yard heads
Barron John, smith, kirkgate
Barrowman John, Baxter, coal hill
Bould Edward, stone-ware merchant, on the shore
Bauld Mrs. stabler, quality-street
Beadie John, corn-merchant, sheriff brae
Beatton William, lint-dresser, dubrow
Beatson Henry, ship master, queen street
Beatson William, ship-master, North Leith
Beatson Peter, ship-master, North Leith
Beatson William, ship-master, queen's street
Begg Will. surveyor of excise, ex warehouse, kirkgate
Begbie Mrs. glazier, tolbooth wynd

Bell and Rannie, wine-merchants, quality ſtreet
Bell Nicol, copper-ſmith, tolbooth wynd
Black Archibald, baxter, tolbooth wynd
Black Mrs. midwife, green tree
Blackhall Alexander, vintner, on the ſhore
Blair Captain, Lee's quarter
Blyth John, officer of exciſe, yard heads
Blyth Colin, ſhoe-maker, walk ſide
Borthwick the right honourable Lady, Springfield
Boſwell David, dancing-maſter, broad wynd
Boſwell Mrs. yard heads
Bowie Edward, taylor on the ſhore
Boyd James, barber, dub-row
Brebner John, wine-merchant, quality ſtreet
Bridie James, merchant, foot of tolbooth wynd
Brough William, merchant, queen ſtreet
Browns Miſſes, yard heads
Brown John, ſhip-maſter, North Leith
Brown John, ſmith, St. Anthon's
Bruce Alexander, vintner, head of the kirkgate
Buchan Thomas, wright, Bernard ſtreet
Buchanan Charles, ſhip-maſter, ſheriff-brae
Buckham William, miniſter, Willy Water's cloſe
Bulloch Andrew, ſhoe-maker, horſe wynd
Burnet Robert, room-ſetter, Bernard ſtreet
Burnet Hugh, confectioner, coal-hill
Burnſide the Rev. William, conſtitution-hill
Butter James, tide-waiter, head of Bernard ſtreet
Bradſhaw Joſeph, vintner, at the golf-houſe

C

Cairns Rob. aſſiſt. regiſter-general of tobacco, ſheriff-brae
Cairns James, wright, yard heads
Campbell Alexander, ſhip-maſter, on the ſhore
Campbell Thomas, officer of exciſe, kirkgate
Caſſels Andrew, ſhip-maſter, Bernard ſtreet
Catanach John, ale-ſeller, on the ſhore
Chalmers James, wine-merchant, citadel
Chalmers Peter, ſhip-maſter, dub-row
Cheap Hugh, wine-merchant, quality ſtreet
Cheyne John and William, ſurgeons, new quay
Chriſtie George, ſtabler, Liddel's cloſe
Chriſtie David, wright, in Kirkgate

P

Christie William, wheel-wright, kirkgate
Clark William, pedlar, foot of Willy Waters' close
Clark Martin, long-gate side
Cleghorns Robert and Alex. baxters, tolbooth wynd
Cleghorn Mrs. citadel
Cleghorn William, baxter, coal-hill
Coulston John, barber, broad wynd
Coke William, bookseller, on the shore
Comb Matthew, sen. brewer, kirkgate
Comb Matthew, jun. porter-brewer, sheriff-brae
Coupar John, painter, tolbooth wynd
Cowan Charles, grocer and tea-dealer, tolbooth wynd
Crawford John, ship-master, coal-hill
Crawford William, merchant, rotten-row
Crichton Mrs. vintner, Bernard street
Crockat Robert, wine cooper, rotten-row
Crockat John, slater, kirkgate
Crookshanks John, vintner, on the shore
Cumming William, vintner, on the shore
Cunningham Mrs. starch-manufacturer, Bernard street
Cundell James and Son, brewers, sheriff-brae
Currie James, ship-master, bridge end
Currie Mrs. vintner, on the shore
Currie Nicol, ship-master, Willy Water's close

D

Dalgliesh John, baker, in queen-street
Dalton Robert, merchant, new quay
Darnie James, taylor, North Leith
Dick John, ship-master, precious close
Dick John, vintner and chaise-hyrer, kirkgate
Dickson Mrs. merchant, on the shore
Dickson John, club-maker, foot of the walk
Dodds Mr. walk side
Doeg David, land-waiter, Willy Water's close
Donaldson David, grocer, on the shore
Douglas William, wine-merchant, Bonyhaugh
Douglas Mrs. broad wynd
Dow James, barber, at the bridge
Dryburgh Robert, ship-builder, North Leith
Drysdale William, corn-merchant, coal-hill
Duff John, room-setter, kirkgate
Duncan John, tobacconist, kirkgate

Duncan Mrs. vintner, on the shore
Durham John, sawer, Liddel's close, dubrow
Dykes William, barber, on the shore

E

Edmonstone William, surgeon, Lee's quarter
Excise ware-house, foot of kirkgate

F

Fairly David, mason, sheriff-brae
Farmer Peter, ship-master, Burges' close
Fenwick John, Esq. easter road
Field George, barber, on the shore
Finlay James, ship-master, old sugar-house close
Finlay Robert, vintner, on the shore
Finlayson Thomas, baxter, tolbooth wynd
Forrester William, ship-master, new quay
Forrester Robert, ship-master, coal-hill
Fortune Alex. leather-merchant, foot of Leith walk
Fortune James, shoe-maker, ditto
Fyfe Barclay, merchant, broad wynd
Fyfe Peter, tolbooth wynd

G

Galletly Andrew, officer of excise, yard heads
Gardiner Harry, grocer, foot of dub-row
Gibb Alexander, tobacconist, tolbooth wynd
Gibson and Anderson, surgeons, broad wynd
Gibson James, last, heel, and paton-maker, kirkgate
Giles Mary and Alexander, brewers, Lee's quarter
Giles Alexander, grocer, dub-row
Gladstones James, school master, North Leith
Gladstones Thomas, flour and barley merch. coal-hill
Glasgow Andrew, porter-dealer, kirkgate
Glass-houses, foot of the links
Golf-house, head of the links
Glover William, merchant, new quay
Gordon James, jun. merchant, kirkgate
Gordon Thomas, Dutch commissary, citadel
Gordon James, wine merchant, quality-street
Gordon John, merchant, on the shore
Gordon Janet, merchant on the shore
Gordon John, land-surveyor, on the shore
Graham John, wine-cooper, quality-street
Graham Hugh, grocer, kirkgate

Grant Duncan, fhip-mafter, bridge-end
Grant John, merchant, Bernard-ftreet
Grant Alexander, lint-dreffer, dub-row
Gray James, fhip-mafter, rotten-row

H

Hadaway Thomas, brewer, yard heads
Hadaway John, wine-merchant, yard heads
Haggart William, wine-merchant, North Leith
Haig Mrs. mantua-maker, on the fhore
Haldane James, vintner, on the fhore
Hall John, fhoe-maker, tolbooth wynd
Halibui ton Campbell, corn-merchant, on the bridge
Hamilton James, fhore-mafter, on the fhore
Hamilton William, wright, Liddel's clofe
Hamilton James, merchant, kirkgate
Hardie George, baker, kirkgate
Hardie John, fhip-mafter, North Leith
Hardie James, fenior, coaft-waiter, kirkgate
Hardie James, junior, grocer, tolbooth wynd
Harris Mrs. oppofite to the green tree
Harley John, vintner, on the fhore
Harley Mrs. vintner, Bernard ftreet
Harper James, candle-maker, tolbooth wynd
Hay Mrs. merchant, on the fhore
Henderfon John, edge-tool maker, kirkgate
Henderfon Alexander, lint-dreffer, dub-row
Henderfon John, fmith, kirkgate
Herdman Robert, ale-feller, tolbooth wynd
Hill Alexander, boat-builder, North Leith
Hogg Thomas, fhip-mafter, North Leith
Hodge James, glazier, queen-ftreet
Home Mrs. of Whitefield, foot of Leith-walk
Horn the honourable general, kirkgate
Hofie John, taylor, Willy Water's clofe
Hume William, fhip-mafter, North Leith
Hume James, fhip-mafter, North Leith
Hunter William, fhip-mafter, dub-row
Hunter and Smith merchants, water-lane
Hutton James, merchant, Bernard ftreet

I

Innes John, merchant, precious clofe
Innes Mrs. foot of kirkgate

Jamiefon John, wine-merchant, rotten-row
Jamiefon John, jun. wine-merchant, rotten-row
Jamiefon John and Co. merchants, timber bufh
Jamiefon and Patten, foap and candle-makers, fher.brae
Johnftone David, minifter, North Leith
Johnftone Thomas, barber, on the fhore

K

Kay David, malt-merchant, dub-row
Keid Thomas, foot of Leith walk
Keir Steven, baxter, head of the long-gate fide
Kelly George, furgeon, tolbooth wynd
Kerr Robert and Co. merchants, on the fhore
Kerr Willam, ftone-ware merchant, Bernard's nook
Kerr Beaumont, fhoe-maker, kirkgate
Kerr Mrs. midwife, kirkgate
Keri William, land-waiter, foot of the fhore
Kidd James, fhip-mafter, on the fhore
King John, houfe and fhip-joiner, on the fhore
Kinnair David, wright, kirkgate
Knox John, taylor, queen ftreet

L

Laidlaw Alexander, meal-merchant, coal-hill
Laing William, baxter, tolbooth wynd
Lamb James, wright, north Leith
Landels Alexander, fhip-mafter, north Leith
Laurie John, fhip mafter, on the bridge
Laverock Mrs. vintner, on the fhore
Lawfon Thomas, vintner, on the fhore
Lawfon James, fmith, kirkgate
Lee James, taylor, dub-row.
Le Grand Mrs. Lee's quarter
Lennox Mrs. vintner on the fhore
Lethem George, barber, tolbooth wynd
Liddle Evan, gardener, fheriff-brae
Liddle John, fhip mafher, north Leith
Liddle Robert, fhip-mafter, north Leith
Liddle Adam, fhip-mafter, coal-hill
Lindfay Gray, collector's clerk, cuftomhoufe, N. Leith
Lindfay Alex. Eng. teacher, and feffion clerk, at pipes
Lindfay James, wine-merchant, quality ftreet
Lithgow Robert, fchool-mafter, old fugar houte clofe

Logan John, minifter, conftitution hill
Low Andrew, wright, Liddel's clofe
Lyon William, wright, queen ftreet
Lyon Peter, fhoe-maker, broad wynd
Lyull William, fhip mafter at Pattons bufh yate

M

Maitland James, fhip-mafter, queen ftreet
Maitland George, vintner, kirkgate
Malloch William, wright, walk-fide
Marfhall William, fhip-mafter, Bernard ftreet
Martin and Ker, merchants, Bernard ftreet
Marble yard in Bernard ftreet
Martin Robert, mafon, tolbooth wynd
Martin William, coaft-waiter, quality-ftreet
Mafon John, mafon, Lee's quarter
Mathiefon Dougal, fhip-mafter, tolbooth wynd
Mathiefon Mrs. vintner, new quay
Maul William, at the links
M'Alhattan John, wright, dub-row
M'Cormack Mrs, kirkgate
M'Culloch David, land-waiter, walk fide
M'Donald James, tolbooth wynd
M'Dougal Dougal Efq, bowling green
M'Glafhan James, grocer, Bernard ftreet
M'Intofh Lady, on the fhore
M'Intyre Mrs, grocer, on the bridge
M'Intyre Patrick, clerk to, and at the glafs-houfe
M'Target Walter, rope-maker, green tree
M'Kenzie Captain, citadel
M'Kerras and Cundell, merchants, Bernard ftreet
M'Laren David, corn merchant, kirkgate
M'Lean John, merchant, in broad wynd
M'Neal Peter, common cryer, queen ftreet
M'Queen James, fmith, Liddel's clofe
M'Vicar William, vintner, on the fhore
Mavine Robert, ftabler, Bernard ftreet
Meldrum John, grocer, Lee's quarter
Melvil Harry, fchool mafter, fheriff-brae
Menzies Captain Alexander, Springfield, Leith walk
Menzies Mrs. vintner, foot of Leith walk
Midcalf Mrs. midwife, kirkgate
Millar Arthur, merchant, Sprinfield

Millar Peter, corn-merchant, sheriff-brae
Millar John, shoe-maker, head of the long-gate side
Mitchell and Sherriff, merchants, links
Mitchell James, brewer, long gate side
Mitchell James, merchant, at the new kirk
Monteith William, grocer, kirkgate
Morison James, marble cutter, horse wynd
Morison James, merchant, opposite the pipes
Morton William, corn-merchant, sheriff-brae
Morton Hugh, wright, kirkgate
Morton Thomas, chaise-hyrer, foot of the shore
Moyse William, wright, Liddel's crofe
Muckle George, wright, Liddel's close
Muckle George, on the shore
Mudie Robert, ship-master, kirk-gate
Mudie Alexander, shore-dues office, broad wynd
Muir John, taylor kirk-gate
Murdock Thomas, pistol-maker, walk side
Muldrup Thomas, stone-ware merchant, and Danish
    consul, timber bush
Morison William, assistant land-surveyor of custom,
    middle of Leith walk
Mudie Mrs. at the bowling-green
Muir David, hop-merchant, on the shore

N

Naesmith Gavin, wright, rotten-row road
Nairn John, vintner, on the shore
Neddery James, taylor, tolbooth wynd
Neilson Alexander, writer, tolbooth wynd
Neilson John, druggist, tolbooth wynd
Neilson Walter, merchant, Springfield
Neilson Gilbert, soap and candle-maker, long-gateside
Neilson and Son, painters, Constitution hill
Neilson David, soap-maker, tolbooth wynd
Nicolson Robert, grocer, kirkgate
Nimmo Andrew, wheel-wright, kirkgate
Norrie George, merchant, on the shore

O

Ogilive David, ship-master, tolbooth wynd
Ogilvie James, ship-master, precious close
Ogilvie Alexander, manager of new roperie, saw-mill

Oliphant David, post-master, Bernard-street
Oliphant William, bulker, Willie Waters' close
Orr James, merchant, on the shore

P

Paisley James, grocer, coal-hill
Paterson Hugh, grocer, sheriff-brae
Paterson George, spade-maker, walk side
Patton Mr. ship-master, shiriff-brae
Paton William, hatter, at the pipes
Paton William, senier, vintner, bush-gate
Pattison John, town-clerk, foot of Kirkgate
Peacock Andrew, tobacconist, on the shore
Pentland Alexander, wine-cooper, quality street
Pew Alexander, wheel-wright, new quay
Philip Charles, merchant, on the shore
Philp John, taylor, tolbooth wynd
Pillans James, merchant, sheriff-brae
Pillans Mr. merchant, Willie water's closs
Pitcaitland David, mason, long-gate side
Pollock's Hugh, cooper, queen's street
Post-office, in Bernard street
Proudfoot John, minister associate congregation, kirkg.
Purcel John, baxter, bridge-end

R

Ramsay George, merchant, kirk gate
Ramsay M'Naughton, ship-master, old sugar house close
Ramsay Williamson & Co. merchants on the shore
Rannie James, junior, merchant, rotton row
Rattrays Miss, of Craig-hall, quality street
Raeburn George, taylor, foot of tolbooth wynd
Reid James, starch-maker, kirkgate
Reid David, Esq. inspector gen. of customs, Springfield
Richardson Mrs. sadler, kirkgate
Ridlay James, merchant, on the shore
Ridlay Magnus, tobacconist, on the shore
Ritchie George, ship-master, broad wynd
Ritchie Alexander, sen. ship-master, broad wynd
Ritchie Alexander, jun. ship-master, on the shore
Ritchie Mrs. vintner, on the shore
Robertson Will. master of Montrose packet, N. Leith
Robertson George, ship-master, on the shore
Robertson Duncan, merchant, quality street.

Roberson and Ronald, merchants, broad-wynd
Robertson Robert, bazter, tolbooth wynd
Robertson William, grocer, on the shore
Rodger David, grocer, coal-hill
Rodger John, baxter, kirkgate
Ronaldson George, baxter, coal-hill
Ross David, ship master, tolbooth wynd
Ross Mrs. vintner, on the shore
Ross and Mathieson, milleners and haberdashers, queen's streeet

S

Scails Adolphus, and Andrew rope-makers, links
Sugar-house, kirkgate
Scott Robert, baxter, queen street
Scott John, shoe-maker, queen street
Scott the reverend Thomas, minister, kirkgate
Scott William, brewer, kirkgate
Scott James, watch-maker, on the shore
Scott Peter, merchant, tolbooth wynd
Scougal John, ship-master, tolbooth wynd
Sherriff Alexander, wine-merchant, sherriff brae
Sherriff Gilbert, ship-master, on the bridge
Sherriff Robert, merchant, Bernard street
Shortried Robert, grocer, dub row
Sibbald William, merchant, opposite the glass house
Sime John, ship-builder, north Leith
Simpson James, wheel-wright, kirkgate
Simspon Daniel, cork cutter, tolbooth wynd
Sinclair Andrew, cork-cutter, kirkgate
Sheay Mrs. foot of Leith walk
Skene John, messenger, kirkgate
Skene Andrew, hair-dresser, kirkgate
Skirving George, ship-master queens street
Smith Thomas, ship-master, on the shore
Smith William, ship-master, north Leith
Smith John, ship-master, head of sherriff brae
Smith Robert, taylor, broad wynd
Smith William, ship-master, on the shore
Smith David, smith, Liddel's close
Smith Robert, preparer of Anderson's pills, Bowie's cl.
Smellie William, and Co. porter sellers, kirkgate

Snelling Mrs, vintner, on the shore
Somervell Patrick, lint-dresser, dub row
Somervell Alex. inspec. for board of trustees, sheriff br.
Steele George, ship-master, on the shore
Stead John and Son, card-makers, walk side
Stevenson David, ship-master, on the shore
Stewart Captain, bowling green
Stewart Archibald, baxter, tolbooth wynd
Stewart John, officer of excise, kirkgate
Stewart John, baxter, sheriff brae
Stoddart Thomas, wood-merchant, saw mill
Strachan Mis long gate side
Strachan William, writer dub-row
Straton Miss, milliner, new quay
Straton William, officer of excise, W. end of Liddel's cl.
Straton Mrs. William, cork-cutter, ditto
Straton Mis yard heads
Strong Lawrence, of the Shetland packet, on the brid.
Strong Robert, and Son, merchants, on the bridge
Strong James, ship-master, walk-side
Sligo John, spirit and tea-dealer foot of broad wynd

E

Taylor Thomas, smith, kirkgate
Thomson James, clerk to the glass house, kirkgate
Thomson John, ship-master, broad wynd
Thomson James, ship-master, tolbooth wynd
Thomson William, ship-master, quality street
Thomson John senior, merchant, sheriff-brae
Thomson John, junior, merchant, quality street
Thomson John, block-maker, queen street
Thomson Robert, shoe-maker, on the shore
Thomson Mrs. vintner, on the shore
Thomson Katherine, vintner, Burges' close
Tod George, ship-master, tolbooth wynd
Tod Richard and Son, wood-merchants, saw mill
Torop Christoper, merchant, new quay
Turnbull and Co. sacking-factory, sherriff-brae
Turnbull John, copper-smith, tolbooth wynd
Thorburn Mrs spirit and teadeler, kirkgate

U

Urquhart Alexander, ship-master, tolbooth wynd

V

Vallentine Mrs, vintner, on the shore
Veitch John, grocer, kirkgate

W

Waddel Alexander tide-surveyor, on the shore
Watt Mrs in broad wynd
Walker Thomas, merchant, queen street
Walker Adam, shoe-maker, kirkgate
Wallace Mrs. barber, tolbooth wynd
Wallace John, malt-merchant, Cableftom's wynd
Watfon James, writer, middle of Leith walk
Watfon John, merchant, new quay
Watfon William, merchant, Bernard street
Watfon Mrs. vintner on the store
Watt William, merchant, queen street
Waugh Thomas, grocer, on the shore
Waugh David, flesher, tolbooth wynd
White Mrs. merchant, rotten row
White Thomas, vintner, on the shore
Williamfon Robert, vintner and chair-hyrer, the shore
Wilfon Thomas, wright, walk-side
Wilfon John, mafter of the grammar school kirkgate
Wood Robert, shoe-maker, tolbooth wynd
Wood Alexander, mathematician, Riddle's clofe
Wood Criftopher, merchant, Bernard street
Wood Hugh, merchant, queen street
Wright James, fmith, St. Andrew
Wright William, nurfery man, links

Y

Yetts John, on the shore
Young James, ship-mafter, rotten row
Young James, brewer, yard heads
Young Patrick, fchool-mafter, broad wynd

LIST of CONSTABLES for 1778.

RObert Allan, merchant, Sun fire office, Writers 'Court, Preses, his bounds begins at north-side of West-port, and up to the head of the West-bow, north-side

Alexander Wilson, merchant, back of Weigh-house, begins at the west-side head of the Bow, and up the south and down the north-side of the Castle-hill to Nairn's close.

Alexander Kedie, candle-maker, Lawn-market, begins at the east-side of Nairn's close, and ends at Gladstone's close.

Robert Aichison, watch-maker, back of the Guard, begins at Gladstone's close, and ends at the undermost Baxters close.

James Haig, merchant, Bow-head, begins at the undermost Baxters close, and ends west-side of Byres's close.

James Myleston, merchant, Exchange, begins at east-side Byre's close, and ends west-side of Allan's close.

James Donald, druggist, opposite to the Guard, begins at the east-side Allan's close, and ends west-side of of Geddes's close.

William Murray, baker, head of the Cowgate, begins at Geddes's close, and ends at Bull's close.

William Hunter, merchant, head of the Cowgate, house Paxton's land, begins at the east-side of Bull's close, and ends west-side of Halkerstone's wynd.

James Carfrae, merchant, front of the Exchange, begins at east-side of Halkerstone's wynd, and ends west-side of Morison's close

Peter Mellis, flesher, Flesh-market, begins at the east-side of Morison's close, and ends west-side of Chalmer's close.

John Howden, sadler, Grass-market, begins at the east-side of Chalmer's close, and ends west side of Leith-wynd.

James Ranken, back of the Boughts, begins at the

weſt-ſide of St Mary's wynd, and up ſouth-ſide
the ſtreet to Blackfriar's wynd.

Robert Laurieſton, merchant, Parliament-ſquare,
houſe Libberton's wynd, begins at the Cowgate-
port, both ſides to Blackfriar's wynd, and eaſt-ſide
of High-ſchool wynd.

John Gray, baker, foot of Caſtle-wynd, begins at the
weſt-ſide of the High-ſchool wynd to the eaſt ſide
of Robertſon's cloſe, including Cant and Dickſon's
cloſes.

Malcolm Wright, merchant, Lawn-market, houſe
head of the Weſt-bow, begins at the head of Kinloch's cloſe to Blackfriars wynd, with Ferguſon's
cloſe and Niddry and Merlin's wynds.

Samuel Gilmor, rope-maker, Graſs-market, begins at
the Iron-church, and ends eaſt-ſide Bell's wynd.

Robert Steele, confectioner, oppoſite to Bridge-ſtreet,
begins at the weſt-ſide of Bell's wynd, and ends
eaſt-ſide of Borthwick's cloſe.

John Aitchiſon, merchant, at the croſs, houſe Allan's
cloſe, begins at the weſt-ſide of Borthwick's cloſe
to Parliament-ſquare and foot of ditto, with Fiſh-
market, and on the north-ſide of the Cowgate to
the kirk-heugh.

Donald M'Lean, merchant, High-ſtreet, oppoſite to
the Croſs-well, begins at the weſt-ſide of the Fiſh-
market, including Parliament-ſquare and ſouth-ſide
of Luckenbooths.

Bernard Henderſon, merchant, Lawn-market, begins
at Haſtie's cloſe, eaſt-ſide of the Horſe-wynd, to
the college and to the Potterrow port.

John Orrock, cutler, High-ſtreet, near the Fountain-
well, begins at the Council-houſe to the eaſt-ſide of
Libberton's wynd, with north-ſide of Cowgate,
from foot of Back-ſtairs to Libberton's wynd.

William Muirhead, bruſh-maker, Lawn-market, Baxter's cloſe, begins at the weſt-ſide of Libberton's
wynd to the head of the Weſt-bow.

David Porteous, painter, Bailie Fyfe's cloſe, begins
at the eaſt-ſide of the Weſt-bow to the Cowgate-

head, including the clofes, and from thence to the north-fide of Libberton's wynd.

John Rae, merchant, Grafs-market, houfe Living-ftone's yards, begins at the Potterrow port, down welt fide of Horfe-wynd, and up fouth-fide of the Cowgate to the Bear-well, and eaft-fide of the Candlemaker-row to the Society.

Ifaac Salter, brewer, college-wynd, begins at the weft-fide of the Society-port, down the weft-fide of the Candlemaker-row to the Cowgate-head, and welt the fouth-fide of the Grafs-market to the Port.

James Clerk, ferrier, back of the Canongate, begins at St Mary's wynd, fouth-fide of the Canongate, to St John's ftreet

Thomas Allan, baker, Canongate-head, begins at St Mary's wynd, fouth fide of the Canongate to St John's ftreet.

LIST of SHERRIFF OFFICERS in and about EDINBURGH.

William Pollock, old affembly clofe
Francis Frafer, lower-moft baxter clofe
William Grant, head of Forrefter's wynd
James Lyon, Morrocco's clofe, lawn market
Grigor Grant, at the crofs
Peter Butter, back of Befs wynd
William Dunlope, portfburgh
Alexander Haftie, at white houfe
William Turner, Giffords park

Country OFFICERS

John Harroway } Dalkeith
Robert Pearie }
James Dixon, Muffelburgh
Samuel M'Dougal, Mid Calder
John Frafer, Weft Calder
Andrew Peebles, Auchendiny
James Mitchell, at Row

( )

George Blackie, at Cranston
George Megget, Nether Libberton.

LIST of the TOWN OFFICERS.

John Braidwood, Bells wynd
William Lindfay, back of mule well, grafs market
Donald M'Kenzie, foot of old fish market clofe
William Fleming, back of Befs wynd
Arthur Forbes bow head
William Begbie, bow head
William Cruckshanks, Befs wynd
Robert Wilfon, Ferlay's clofe, foot of Bell's wynd
Walter Forrester, at the weft port
John Dalrymple, foot of Borthwick's clofe
William Williamfon, near the chapel of Eafe
Malcolm M'Dermed, at the back of the wrights houfes

L E T T E R S

F O R

WILLIAMSON'S

P E N N Y - P O S T.

ARE taken in by Himfelf, at the fign of the lanth
luckenbooths, where Letters are difpatched ei,
times every day to Leith, and as often from then
to Edinburgh and Suburbs, letters circulating within
the city, and at a moderate diftance, are delivered
every hour and oftner.
By Mr William Carnochan, grocer, St Andrew's ftr.
Mr John Campbell, grocer, oppo St John's ftreet can.
Mr William Milne, grocer, Gray and Gibfon's land,
Nicolfon's ftreet
Mr Adam Scotland, grocer, foot of college wynd

( )

Mr James Anderson, grocer, head of Chalmers close

Mr John Andrew, grocer, head of the uppermost entry to James court

Mr William Ramage, grocer, middle of the west port

Mr Andrew Livingstone, lint-manufacturer, and grocer, cowgate head

Mrs Wardrop grocer, foot of castle wynd, grass mar.

Mrs Betty Samuel, grocer, head of fish market close facing the cross

Mrs Cunningham, coffee house, bristo-street

Mr George Maitland, vintner, h. of kirkgate Leith

Mr Thomas Wallace, grocer, kirkgate

Mr Bell, copper-smith, tolbooth wynd

Mrs Ross, on the shore

PORTABLE PRINTING PRESSES

With all the Apparatus belonging them, made and sold by the Publisher, on a short notice: likewise, all the necessary instructions are given, for Composing the Types, imposing the Forms, &c.

This Machine is so constructed, that it will throw off one Folio Page, or Four Quarto Pages at a time, with great ease and exactness.

CPSIA information can be obtained
at www.ICGtesting.com
Printed in the USA
LVOW04s1322080517
533715LV00008B/119/P